Bosses

The artist as receiver, giver, inquisitor, communicator. Leung's writing is emotional and profound, engaging both the very personal and the mundane, the practical and the political. Few artists dig deep into themselves like this: an extraordinary insight into the process of producing art. —Cosey Fanni Tutti

Artist as (girl) boss or maverick scab? The labour–gender question doesn't stay put. Dialectics here grow as wildly and recursively as Ballardian botany. Leung ranges things seen, felt, sensed, thought and made against watertightness as form or as politics. The more gaps, the more space to remake reality. —Marina Vishmidt

I would call Bosses *auto-factual. Leung accounts for work and life co-authored with facts, conjuring a prosaic and beautiful sociality. Her negations are profound, they hold and express the social apophatically. What is not here almost feels like a choice, and the thing convulses.* —Ed Atkins

Some events you can never correct. One of them is childbirth. If you want to know, here it is. —Fanny Howe

Ghislaine Leung

Bosses

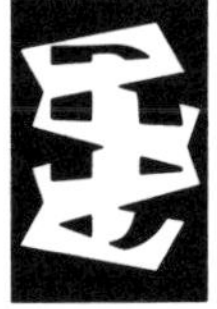

DIVIDED

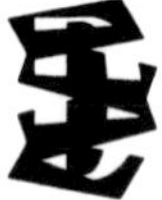

Published in the United Kingdom by Divided in 2023

Divided Publishing
Avenue Louise 251
Level 2, Magistrat side
1050 Brussels
Belgium

Divided Publishing
Deborah House
Retreat Place
London E9 6RJ
United Kingdom

https://divided.online

This book was made with financial support from Museumsverein Abteiberg e.V., Mönchengladbach, the School of Arts and Humanities, Goldsmiths, University of London, and Fluxus Art Projects.

Museumsverein
Abteiberg e.V.

All images from Ghislaine Leung, 'Portraits', Museum Abteiberg, Mönchengladbach, 3 June–24 October 2021, prolonged until 21 November 2021. Courtesy of the artist and Maxwell Graham/Essex Street, New York and Cabinet, London. Photos: Achim Kukulies. All works Museum Abteiberg collection, purchase of the Supporters Circle at Museumsverein Abteiberg, 2022.

This reprint of *Bosses* was made on the occasion of Ghislaine Leung's solo exhibition as part of *from 6:12 pm to 5:48 pm*, curated by Alejandro Alonso Díaz at Espai13. Fundació Joan Miró, Barcelona, July 2026.

Designed by Alex Walker
Printed by Printon, Tallinn

ISBN 978-1-91-642500-2

Some people used to look at all that glitter and say how tacky it looked. We never figured out till much later on that it was simply that most of us were nearsighted. —Martin Wong

I'm tired of hiding everything about it all. Hiding becomes intolerable at some point. My desire to mask my situation is a disadvantage to the understanding of the work. Love is an action, it is learnt, and must be maintained. You are my heart in the world, you told me. I did not know how to love, or I had forgotten. Freedom is often conflated with autonomy, but dependence is perhaps less the incarcerator than the liberator. I am free with support, not without. I am big and you are small, you say. But I am as dependent as you are and this is not an issue because care exists socially, is required and reciprocated a thousand times over in a moment. That I fail to acknowledge this is the price I pay when I misattribute agency to individual life, as identity in a monological sense, in my vivid financialised disincorporated life. Because love is not romance but trust. And trust is not an attribute of the adult.

I felt you before I heard you. Heard you before I saw you. Felt the heavy purple pull and drag of birth, the force of push and tugged life. So short and numb and bright with lights and people. Do I remember you placed at my chest, the familiarity of your entirely new body pulsing and turning in the air? Resting on the fattened darkened breasts still dry and vast. I remember the tiny plastic band on your small dark wrist, its white rigid form against your skin. I remember the hat I bought for you put on your head, browning blood staining the cream knitted wool surface as it covered your matted hairs. I remember it was morning and it felt as if we had surfaced from some enormous and never-ending pool of darkened labour, and were held still for a minute in the shift to light on the new year's day. I remember posing for a photo with you, two photos, self-consciously, thinking that I should allow myself to smile with my teeth, unsure as to which smile was more ingenuous, looking at the camera, not looking at you. Being happy and wanting to be happy and being terrified. I held you because I didn't know how not to, how to put you down, or change you or feed you or comfort you. I felt I did not know how. Did not trust myself to not know well. Wanted your father to rest and sent him away, and was left with you and your grandmother, arriving as scared and old as you. She fed me little chunks of apple cut up. I did not sleep, you did not feed. The evening came and darkened sweaty fetid radiator heat, your father returned and you began to sob and sob while he held you, while I tried to feed you. You sobbed all night and we didn't sleep. And you sobbed in the morning and we packed and left and went home, and you sobbed and we were home in the small darkness of the world before you. And we ate and went to bed and I held you against my breast and nothing came out, and you tried so hard to eat and suck at the nothing until the nipples were cut and bruised and we did not sleep. And I sung over and over and he would take you and rock you and you sobbed. And your guts worked and he changed you, the drying cord that had kept us together held fast with its little white plastic clip. And you sobbed and you did not pass urine and you were so hungry and we called and asked and called and questioned and called and went back, you sobbing. And into the tiny-children's A&E where they weighed you and checked you, alert and angry, lighter than when you left. And into the worst room, the tiny narrow room, where we undressed you and laid you on the paper towels, and you cried. And we held you and they put needles in your small thin heels and into cardboard trays, and nothing came out of you easily. And I thought I would die and rip my own face off, or explode with pain and hate for myself for letting you down. And they gave you formula to drink and you absorbed it like life into your body, falling finally full asleep. And they pushed a catheter up inside you and a tiny stream of urine came out. And I felt my mind break. And they gave you more formula and told us how to feed you and burp you, patting and rubbing on your small back. And alone in the bathroom I failed to recognise the creature that stared back at me from the mirror. You finally slept and we slept and they gave us a feeding schedule and it felt like some kind of hope, something to follow. He made the formula and fed you and I just stopped I think, gave up, not on you, but on myself. And they pumped my dry breasts and nothing came. I felt all I could do was damage maybe. And they told me to drink teas and eat iron. And we went home and I felt like my skin was burning on the inside and like my heart was pumping too hard and that I wasn't really there. And they took my blood pressure and I cried because I had to go in again and I wasn't well and I left to go there alone and the blood wouldn't come out of my veins and the world fizzed. And your grandmother came and stroked my head as I lay without you on the paper-towelled bed. And I felt like nothing, not myself, not with you, wrong and stitched and scared like a child. And I went home and was given drugs and I tried so hard to relax and to love you but my mind was broken by guilt and fear and I could only think that I would hurt you, and I would feel as if I couldn't breathe or I was lost. And I would try to feed you and look at the millilitres of food going in, the substance coming out, but not at you. I couldn't look at you, because all I could see was my own self-hate and fear. And I held you and you ate and slept and we continued. And your father went back to work and your grandmother came and she couldn't work the cooker or the kettle and whatever fear I fed her she doubled. And so she left and we were alone and maybe I called you your name, a little at first and maybe you weren't the baby, maybe you were you. And the spring came and I began to work again because I knew how to work and didn't know how to mother. And I started talking to someone and had so much hate and fear in me, and felt again like a child, and was scared of that. The summer came and we walked for hours under the umbrella and friends came and it helped a little. The waves of hate and guilt for myself never left, they would emerge in the peace of an afternoon or night, thoughts that I would hurt you, the ways I would hurt you, the pain as I would recoil each time at the thought and then think it again. And you would smile and begin to laugh and I would hope sometimes that I would get better. And I worked and worked and tried to forget the pain but it was there. The shame and guilt at my own fear of loving you, thinking my love had hurt you, thinking and hating myself for not trusting my own instincts to care for you. Not seeing that all I had to do to exit that hate, that fear, was trust myself, as simply as you trust me.

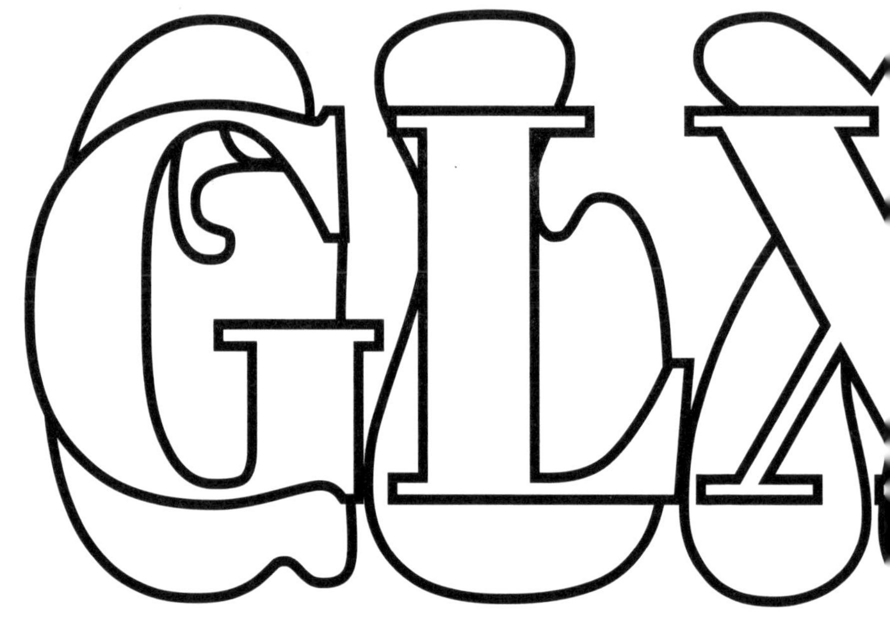
GLX

I subtract. It is a reverse engineering, to circulate and distribute extant conditions in different ways. To make work that is non-singular in its identity, that is contingent, present tense; materials and means that rest upon each other. It is not more than what it is, and, in being that, it is already more than expected. The secret, as the artist Hanne Darboven pointed out, is that there is no secret.

1. 'I don't know what my work is. I have to wait to hear that from someone.' —David Hammons.* To commit to making art is to maintain a somewhat clunky and unverifiable labour form: counter to the dominant logics of proficient margins and executable gains, working without knowing is perhaps a more constitutive factor. What might be understood here as non-productivity is about more than not making. It is an acknowledgement of all the work that goes into the means of distribution, exchange and consumption which is inseparable from production. Services, administration and so on.† As Artist Placement Group stated, 'Context is half the work.' This is not limited to a place or site, it is discourse, histories and community.

* Kellie Jones, 'Interview: David Hammons', *Art Papers* 12:4 (July–August 1988).

† See Andrea Fraser, 'How to Provide an Artistic Service: An Introduction', paper presented at The Depot, Vienna, October 1994.

2. '*Dropout Piece* is the hardest work I have ever done . . . It involved destruction of (or at least complete understanding of) powerful emotional habits.' —Lee Lozano.* The desire to be accommodating, though at first glance generous, often falls into proprietary logics. Giving space is conflated with filling it. I heard a story a long time ago that the artist Gerhard Richter kept a sign on his desk next to his phone that said NO. For a while some years ago I had a SAY NO alarm on my phone that went off every morning at 10 a.m. The habit of wanting to please is often commensurate with conservatism. It is frictionless, not fluid. It is, much like liking, not at all the same as loving.

3. 'In painting you start with a blank canvas, you start with nothing and you create your image, particle by particle; whereas in film, usually, you just open your lens and you have a vast quantity of objects which become parts of your image. They are opposite processes.' —George Landow, AKA Owen Land.† I've always taken photographs. I took photographs all through the period when I stopped taking photographs. Taking a photo is already editorial: you make choices about what not to take. The American writer Mary Robison has often spoken of her rejection of the label 'minimalist': 'I detested it. Subtractionist, I preferred. That at least implied a little effort. Minimalists sounded like we had tiny vocabularies and few ways to use the few words we knew. I thought the term was demeaning; reductive, clouded, misleading, lazily borrowed from painting and that it should have been put back where it belonged.'‡ Subtraction, as opposed to minimalism, infers an editorial process that isn't about having less material but removing more. A maximal subtraction.

4. 'Two basic systems: development and maintenance. The sourball of every revolution: after the revolution, who's going to pick

* Lee Lozano, *Notebooks 1967–70* (New York City: Primary Information, 2010), entry for 5 April 1970.

† P. Adams Sitney, 'Interview with George Landow', *Film Culture* 47 (summer 1969).

‡ Maureen Murray, 'Mary Robison', *Bomb* 77 (autumn 2001).

up the garbage on Monday morning?' —Mierle Laderman Ukeles.* I was reading an interview with the artist Mierle Laderman Ukeles the other day and she was talking about her work *The Keeping of the Keys: Maintenance as Security* (1973), part of her *Maintenance Art Performances* series. In the interview she makes this really great point on collusion: the guards had all the keys, but they didn't use them.† Access can be often be understood as being about having keys, or disseminating keys. There is a feeling that you need keys to get into things, because the things themselves are territories, locked, demarcated and defended. So of course keys are needed. It doesn't have to be this way though. The properties of a thing don't have to be understood as locked enclosures or portfolio real estate. They can be homes. Access, like much else, is something that needs be maintained.

5. 'It is nothing else than one big panel, eighteen small ones, three coloured bulbs and a room. About people who are watching something and courageously start interpreting it. Thus not giving any hope.' —Jef Geys.‡ I have long had a huge affection for synopses, and more specifically descriptions, especially of the conditions of used books, or any in-depth material listing. In being so heavy-handed in their literalism, these descriptions avoid the prescriptive. They say everything and nothing at all. Counter to expectation, the more and larger and more expansive the description, the less clear it becomes. The literal deals with the *is* of things, not the *as*. To feel things in their present and material tense is a difficult and active task. As Gregg Bordowitz wrote, quoting Ian White, 'Look at the leaf. It is not dead as in nothing. It is yellow. Or red. Or even if it is brown it is still not

* Mierle Laderman Ukeles, 'Manifesto for Maintenance Art, 1969! Proposal for an Exhibition: "Care"', 1969.

† 'Mierle Laderman Ukeles in Conversation with Mathieu Copeland', in *The Anti-Museum: An Anthology*, edited by Mathieu Copeland and Balthazar Lovay (London: Koenig Books, 2017), 485–99.

‡ From a photograph of a photocopy of a 1979 Geys text – 'Yellow, Red, Blue, Etc. . . .' – shown to me in a bar in Paris in 2017.

no-colour. Look at the colour. The colour is real, it is something to do and it can be done. War is over IF YOU WANT IT. WANT IT. These are acts.'*

6. 'Does anyone have any questions? I changed my mind, I have no questions. That's it for the broadcast, thank you very much.' —Trisha Donnelly.† The term 'shedding light' is often used in the context of explanatory texts. It is always the object this light is being shed on that is talked about, and not so often the light itself, which of course is open to all sorts of variation and angle, raking and temperature. I have dozens of photos I have tried to take of some weird thing in the inside of my mouth using the flash on my phone, or sometimes a combination of torch and flash, both held awkwardly in one hand. In order to see some little fleshy nodule or chewed bit of mouth. And the photos are invariably over- or under-exposed or blurry or at the wrong angle. Illumination is perhaps not the same as more light, it is often something that happens in and because of the dark.

Why do I seek to exploit myself? I often choose to be my own bad boss. There is a paradox in this situation. Given that I am my own worst enemy, why can't I stop seeking to collude or even be complicit in these abuses? In pulling these labour conditions of exploitation into my own body, I became interested, in an expanded socio-political sense, in what it is not only to put up with our own exploitation, but even to love our own captor. A sort of Stockholm syndrome. The insidious ways in which we justify and validate harm and self-harm. Not only as individuals but as organisations. Specifically in the ways in which we seek to assimilate to and internalise conditions of high production, efficacy and visibility over maintenance and care. Then we've

* Gregg Bordowitz, 'Minus Signs', paper delivered on the occasion of The Ian White Lecture, London, 2 December 2016.

† Trisha Donnelly, 'Conversations with Contemporary Artists Series', MoMA, New York City, 10 November 2016.

succeeded in being that kind of self, and that self passes and succeeds in what is understood as a meritocratic social construct. Thinking on my own labour, I wanted to think of ways that my work could address this not only through striking against my own self-exploitative tendencies, but actively cancelling them. To think of these as constitutive issues of labour connected to market viability, visibility and metrics. A privileging of visibility that compounds extractive forms of production and rides slipshod over informal or invalidated labours and communities. Against this priority of visibility, canonisation inclusive, I became interested, less in making visible, and so the cycle continuing, than in making palpable. In the ways in which informal and non-productive labours might be maintained. I began to stop speaking about labour relations in these terms and began to attempt to labour on these terms. Active as opposed to passive cancelling in sound, for example, works to subtract via addition. You cancel a sound with a sound. This only works in a perfect, closed system, such as in headphones. In an open system it does not work, there are too many variables, it cancels, clashes and moves around. This is where ambiguity is. Active cancellation can also occur in masking. This doesn't block sound but layers it, creates another sound as a foil to conceal the first.

Plain flour
2 × unsalted butter
Caster sugar
Buttermilk
2 × full-fat block cream cheese
Icing sugar
Red food colouring
Caffeine coffee
Broccoli
Cauliflower
Green beans
Cabbage
Avocado
Peas

Cheese
Goat cheese
Lentils
Anchovies
Yoghurt
Corn thins
Crackers

When did I mistake a person for an object, a property for a home, exploitation for liberty?

7.00 change and breast 60ml
8.00 bottle 120ml
10.00 snack 60ml and sleep
11.00 change and breast 30ml
11.40 bottle 120ml
1.00 snack 60ml and sleep
2.00 change and breast 30ml
2.40 bottle 120ml
4.00 snack 60ml and sleep
5.00 change and breast 30ml
5.40 bottle 120ml
7.00 snack 60ml and sleep
8.00 change and breast 30ml
8.40 bottle 120ml
10.00 snack 60ml and sleep
11.00 change and dream feed 90ml

5 × 120ml
1 × 90ml
4 × 30ml
6 × 60ml

Wondrous tiny frame and weightless heavy limbs, tongue nested in unshod jaws. Lolling. The off ashen acrid scent of labour. Risk can be re-understood in this context as our dependency on, and care of, the collective body. This stands in stark opposition to the cultural prioritisation of for-profit speculative models of individualised financial independence. Such models exploit the porous and interdependent tissue of the social body. In order to access this exploitation we must also be part of it. So this exploitation is, in fact, a self-exploitation on a grand and all-pervasive scale. Counterintuitively the many do not outweigh the few, as the few are part of the many. Sacrifice, the imperative to continue, to push, against all odds, to risk life and limb for others is nullified if we question the binary it stands on, if we are others. A body is not comprised of identical elements, or even only human elements, it is an infrastructure of dependency. A social body is likewise constituted by a raft of soft foldings into multiple groups and groupings. Self-care is social care, not because everyone is looking after themselves but simply because we are each other. The arc of the head, curved and warm-nebulous, the ubiquitous smell of earth, and dirt and life, mouth-shaped, pulsing and inaccurate. Thin hairs that coat, lustrous and sparse, more felt than seen. I spent a long time trying to expunge the pronoun 'we' from my writing. What 'we' was I writing for, who was I claiming to speak on behalf of? The onus is on finding your own voice in order to stake out a ground. It implies a singularity of perspective no one could totally claim to have. Not even the lonely. Especially the lonely.

We are possessed my love, possessed.

7.00 wake bottle change
8.00 play
8.30–9.15 nap
10.00 bottle change
10.15/11.00 nap
11.00 walk
11.30/12.00 nap
1.00 bottle change
2.00 walk
2.30/3.00 nap
4.00 bottle change

5.00 story time
5.30/6.00 bath change
7.00 bottle bed
10.30 dream feed change 90ml
5.00 bottle change

It's about being too close, proximate and thigh-deep as a form of lived embodied critique. A kind of low performance. Writing and rewriting structures, architecture and organisation. Working with new and wild, highly subjective forms of regulation against objectivising deregulated neoliberal for-profit algorithms. Liveness, generative practices. Acknowledging the relation between the individual and the group. Context, the situation around a thing, so less a thing but a material event. Unless all of us are free none of us are free. Fundamentally re-inscribing what liberty is outside of individual liberties. It's about the capacity to notice how things are and as such imagine how they could not be as they are. Agency isn't just privilege or merit, it is the very reality of our imaginative capacity, and the labour required to maintain those resistive acts. We need to regulate against those that would exploit us, including the policing internalised in ourselves, and we need to do that by wresting back our liberties, fought for, maintained, unknown and yet to fight for, from a totalitarian and insidious free-market neoliberalism.

23.20 cough vomit food, had water
Rest
23.50 cough vomit food
Rest
00.10 cough vomit liquid
Rest
00.32 vomit liquid 36.5C cold sweat
Sleep
00.55 gagging vomit small liquid sweaty
Sleep
1.25 gagging vomit small liquid sweaty
Sleep

2.05 retching small liquid
Sleep
3.05 retching small liquid
Sleep
3.55 retching small liquid
Sleep
5.10 wanted water threw it up
Little sips tolerated
6.15 sick small liquid
Little sips water
9.30 half banana
10.30 little bit of bread no crusts

The space around me that isn't you. The soft murmur of radio four walls apart from me. The waistband of my jeans curving into my stomach. The heat of my own body reflected back against me, moving in my breath. The soft burr and dull ache of engines expelling fuel into the sky. The bend of my nape and gravity of my body here without you. The flash of sirens and humming and the shape of my newly cleaned teeth. The space of a time not yet assigned and weighty in potential, light in actuality. The sets of minutes that frame. The constant assessing of my own ineffectuality tied to some misconstrued fairy tale of achieving. Time that is mine moves away and was never mine. It is the speculation on the use of time that obliterates space. Not only in the metric benefit but the profit yield of that metric. The gains, again the gains. And so the losses. And held somewhere close to the spine the knowledge of the importance of something other than this playing field. Something as still and dull and newborn as the present.

Snub-nosed matt-black ballerina pumps, the side of a tiny black invisible mini-sock running parallel to the side of the shoe and against the skin. Two flattened black bows, one on each shoe, never untied and purposeless save as decoration. The tips of the shoes touch and form a small defence around a bag. The bag, small, black and emblazoned in different typeface styles with capitalised words such as FRIENDS and DRINKS.

Imagine loving and having loved that ear, pink, long, lobeless. A small colourless mole at its apex adjoining the face.

An index finger and thumb moving over the skin of his fingers, tearing at chunks of skin and scab on the red welts below each nail. Tiny fragments of broken skin pulled off and discarded and then the raw end found again and pulled. The hands settling, stopping, only to begin the process again with a light caress along a surface, and then the pulling and tearing on new grounds.

A Longchamp bag, stacked espadrilles, small gold hoops, a small crescent-moon tattoo behind the ear. The book is an express guide to law.

A DKNY tote in claret, a black wrap coat, an engagement ring, flat black pumps and tights.

A KFC Pepsi cup held in the hand at the same time as a small succulent plant.

Badly painted gloss-white fingernails.

A constant running background replay of events now unfolded, which I can do nothing to alter. A gelled continuity of minor errors and dumbnesses to be recounted, punctuated by moments of nausea or hunger or panic over some other issue temporarily given higher grounds of attention or fear.

The scent of peeling citrus fruit. Imagining zest spraying visually in the air and carrying to the face and nose and entering the respiratory system. This zest could equally be a cough or stale mouth scent or petrol or warm skin.

The nausea is constant, apart from when it departs bringing on the rapidly forming foregone conclusions of worse ailments signalled by this turn. To feel sick and simultaneously tired as a constant. Within a few weeks I cannot remember how it was otherwise, or I cannot remember otherwise.

A card game on a small screen held in the hand. Point of view shows three figures engaged in the game and your hand. The figures are caricatures, heads expanded maybe twenty per cent, unmoving, facial features pulled large, noses particularly, perhaps also chins in some cases. The head attached to the arm holding this game has hair styled from the crown of the head, soft and straight, curling only at the edges framing the face. The neck tan and soft and thin, the stubble close-shaven and dark.

Purple-green-veined iridescent monstrous or ugly or beautiful leaves. Some curled down like claws or cupped, either growing or dying and both. Clustered on top of each other and magenta underneath, textured skin thin on tender hairy stems.

Luminescent pink-tinged white blossom heads like paper coming out from impossible buds and the sugar scent of jasmine over road noise and a thick calm in the body, or stagnant water.

Depression is symptoms that are in and of themselves depressing. Not rational or relatable, the condition is one of alienation, that of the body in actuality, flesh and life. It is not a refusal to live or move, but that living and moving are, and only are. The desire to OFF, to turn off this weight, sometimes felt as agency that horseshoes in on itself to the equally moribund and actual.

This simple manoeuvre of turning, of moving from one position to another. Rotting with festering mouldy leaves and a tiny new base growth. Blight as a condition of living and living well, inclusive.

This overwhelming love of specific animal groups. Frenzied identification and appreciation of types. I don't get it.

Time no longer for anything, too late to organise filler activities, it is not extractable.

Black nylon sports bottoms, a heavily patterned shirt, phone in hand, hand in pocket.

Skin-tight denim-blue zip-backed Lycra pencil skirt, spaghetti-strapped black vest and pink headscarf.

Two large tears stationary on the cheeks at the end of fast drying salt tributaries.

Two hats and sandals and socks as a combo.

Contra most narratives on fertility, the doubling of life does not feel like health but sickness. It is in its utmost living quality that it feels as death, as age, as illness. No picture of vitality, shuffling, too slow and in too many clothes to register.

A dim room, a dry mouth. Orange-blue light streaking to mid-grey on a wall, the sound of covers moving, the nothing temperature scent of your own body, the weight of skull, soft ache of a limb.

Dyed red-brown or auburn hair, thin and white at the roots and scalp skin, fluffing and covering the surface of the head. Ruggedly folded swathes of ear skin embossed with azure pearl-stud earrings. Topped off with a pink fleece and cross-body bag that cuts and compounds the fleece layer insinuating a smaller form. The hair cusps the fleece neck.

Going through the bag, moving objects into pockets zipped and checked. Patted for security and rechecked for accuracy.

'I think it's painting. I'm not too fond of painting. I find it so— I'm not as good at dealing with it.'

A Barbour jacket with a pink shirt worn collar-up, the whole affair stretched taut over a vast frame, and inhabited to its full structural capacity.

I ate a falafel wrap, no onions, two chillies, and walked home to throw it up.

Real estate opportunities abound.

Two thin royal-blue carrier bags, handles shaped by their own weight. The scene held between jean legs ending in fabric Adidas trainers that point out and away from each other.

Orange roses.

ANIMA 07588 733 111.

Crossed at the ankle, crossed at the knee, crossed at the ankle. Left to right.

The portion of toe or toes that shunts forward in a sandal and overhangs the front edge, curving over a platform or trailing in the dirt ahead of the shoe. It repulses him.

Up your game
Stop switching
Trust

Any window with a hammer is an exit.

Includes tape, cards, dying flowers, dirty rained-on soft toys and small offerings of alcohol.

Dreams. The bed specialist.

IT IS WHAT IT IS

A feeling, a speed perhaps. It was muscular, the feel-good of a stretch. It was not perfunctory because it had no function to perform. There are the times when touching that are felt as scenarios, positions, partners, techniques, visual and ideological, and there are other times. I suspect only one is love.

One roll of toilet paper, one tub of Coffee-Mate, one large jar of instant coffee, one banana, all in a bag that states Don't be too jolly.

A giant stuffed teddy bear, human-sized, replete with cardboard sign, made by its owner, that reads HOMELESS PLEASE HELP.

Anxiety is after all nothing but something and a surplus of rationales. Where reason overloads itself, reason after reason after reason, all countering themselves, compounding themselves. It is first and foremost, secondly and lastly, the desire for reasons. The over-reasoned, those without, or unable not to attempt to comprehend, faith.

At the dinner. And it was *the* dinner, definite article, not *a* dinner, or just *dinner*, but *the* dinner as attributable only to dinners belonging to specific events, say weddings, openings, galas and other things attended. At the dinner, the older woman, who had worked in some capacity in patronage or management, encouraged talking to the statesman. He, historical and drunk, was holding court, having arrived late to the dinner. Later, attempting perhaps to kiss, the sodden dry tongue hitting my turned cheek, everyone was embarrassed, save him, drunk and historical, embarrassed of him, us, for themselves to feel this way at all, to feel at all. Which is why it all ever happens. And the refrain continues.

It is always two become one. Far less is said about one becoming two, and most of what is said is monstrous.

The interior walls of the plane are not white or grey-white or off-white but white with thin diagonal grey uneven stripes extending at an angle just short of forty-five degrees. There is no trace of repetition in the pattern, it is perhaps not a pattern.

Two seats across from me a woman in a cap-sleeved black fabric top with black lace panels is watching the live-action version of Dumbo. I gather this from only one scene of a small elephant which then cuts to a woman. The elephant is melancholy, tearful and babyish with an expressive snout, the woman vaguely villainous and Victorian and I can see a circus-like tent structure in the background. It could be a documentary, but the colours are of the wrong saturation and density. Now the melancholy elephant is perched atop a revolving stage. Confused looks pass between figures apparent as authority. The woman is watching, her head resting on the hard yellow back of the seat in front.

I'll say it again, it is my favourite thing to swim naked in the dark, blind and blurred, not only myself and all shattered fluid into stars and salt water.

No Connection.

A cola bottle or small pink opaque shrimp or tiny blind white-chocolate mouse. One penny. A penny crime. Nothing.

The taste of sugar gelatine held in the mouth and teeth and gone.

An abandoned VHS boxset entitled *The Civil War*.

The definition of horse-faced.

Assimilation is a violence.

Celebratory Flu Bunting.

Passing is also dying.

A greed for the redeemability of people, of all things.
Like coupons.

History is a dependent.
CALVIN KLEIN
CALVIN KLEIN
CALVIN KLEIN
CALVIN KLEIN
8 November Twenty Nineteen.

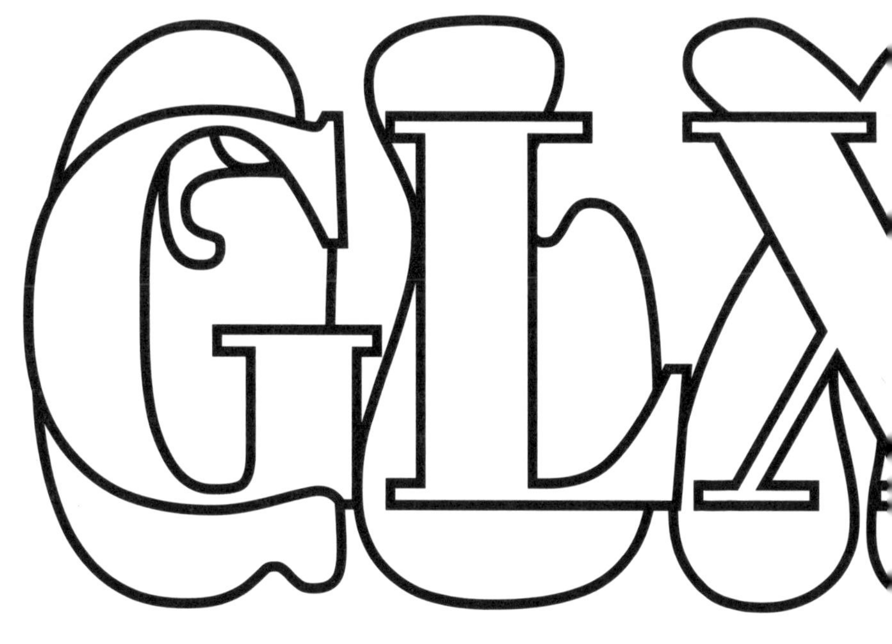

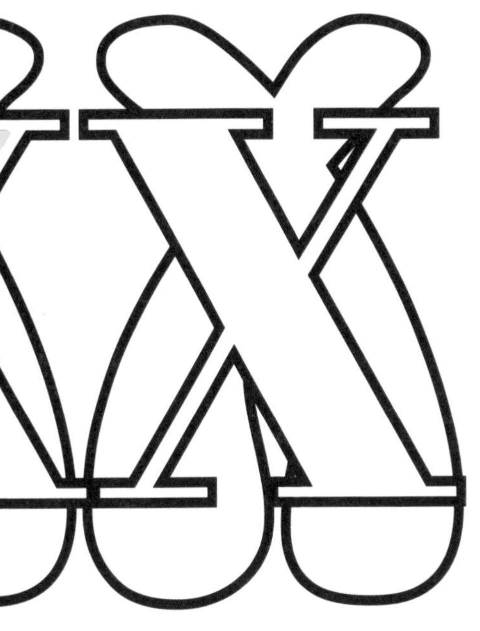

My previous writing delineated a zone to deal with, by what it omitted. Notice how close you can go in before you hit the boundaries set by fear. The fear that turns you towards conservatism.

'Portraits'
Ghislaine Leung
Museum Abteiberg, Mönchengladbach, Germany
3 June–24 October 2021

Arches, 2021
Score: A white inflatable welcome arch in all available rooms

Browns, 2021
Score: All available walls painted in brown to standard picture-hanging height

Daughters, 2021
Score: A children's necklace stapled to the wall

Institutional Drawings, 2021
Drawings on sugar paper

Onions, 2021
Framed oil painting

Portraits, 2021
Title sign

So here we are.* I couldn't travel to Germany until now because of COVID. I knew the Museum Abteiberg but the whole process of this exhibition happened entirely remotely, I didn't even make a site visit after the invitation. This is the first time I have seen the exhibition, four months after its opening. Friends who live nearby have seen it, pictures and documentation have circulated, before I have seen it for myself.

I have a certain way of working with scores. I write a score as a parameter of how a particular work gets shown. I produced this way of working specifically because I was interested in finding a mode of production that made space for a different kind of work, a different way of working for me – something that was generative, that I could do while letting life be what it actually is. A different way of working that could be a long-term practice for me, generative instead of being against my own limitations.

And this comes from something I probably initially conceived of as a problem. I always thought that you can make an artwork, and you can perfect it in some way yourself. And then the work goes into its context, a context that you can't control, and it has a different read or it changes or it shifts. And this was something I wanted to control. It was the wish to control that seemed a clear problem to me. Trying to create light locks or sound locks, to stop video and sound work bleeding for example, fortifying and padding the space, making a false autonomous, independent space for the work so it can float. Blocking out everything else and trying to create perfect conditions for a work, trying to control the environment. I wondered how to embrace the contingency of works instead, to embrace their vulnerability. Rather than thinking, How can I fix this and control this? How can I maintain its integrity in the way that I have conceived it?, I shifted to thinking that the agency or the identity of the work could

* What follows is adapted from a transcript of a discussion I had with Susanne Titz, the director of Museum Abteiberg, Mönchengladbach, on 2 October 2021.

come from its vulnerability, its total contingency, its complete reliance and dependency. Trust in a situation.

Another part of why I started circulating work like this is because I worked at LUX in London. LUX was set up to support moving-image artists by ensuring them fees for screenings. The discussion around video and performance was about how to get a work circulating, questions about where is the work, where is the identity of the work, artist labour, how to edition the work. That was very interesting to me. I was very curious about how to take some of those questions around the identity of an object and its repetition. I wondered if there was a way I could circulate sculpture using this operational structure, and a score was a way I could do that. I would never *show* the score, the point is to *do* the score. I was also interested in how the score was analogous to music structure, and the relationship between composition and musician. You have a piece of music that exists in notation form and then you have the performance of that piece of music. Which one is the work? They are both the work. They are interdependent and that is interesting. It gets the work out of sole authorship, it questions fixed objecthood or identity, because the identity of the work is always held in the question of interdependency.

At times there has been a push-back because collaborating with an institutional space that is displaying my work almost becomes about trying to make them accountable or trying to make them show their own hand in the production. And this is very often pushed back against because it seems to be something that people don't want in general. The score is not an idea or a material, it's from my conditions of life. The critique is about how I institute, introduce it into the institution; that does change it. For example, if I only work three days a week, that changes how they work. It is largely assumed to be the artist's role to make decisions of production – the gallery is like, Just tell us how to do it, just make those decisions. Although a lot of material is already there and a lot of decisions for the way an artist can work are already defined. Even though I have these scores, it'll still come down to, Actually, can you come? Actually, can you just make the decision? But there's no way that the work should look. I don't want to police the life out of myself and the work, the work is learning to trust and not to know, and not to see this as a compromise for the exhibition.

I didn't have those requests with Museum Abteiberg, because I couldn't come because of COVID and it's the first time that the scores have had to work so hard. And there's had to be a lot of trust and collaboration through the engine of the score. It's produced something that surprises me. So coming and seeing the show in person today felt like coming to see . . . a show. It's interesting, I truly do not feel that I entirely made it, I feel this was made with somebody else. It is not the sole production of me, executed by somebody else. It's definitely something that has come together and been generated not only by me, but by Susanne, by the space, by the history, by the contemporary conditions; all of these contingencies utterly to the fore. All of the limits are material in this show.* And it's actually quite challenging, in an authorial sense, to see that now, it's harder than I thought it would be, it's challenging to the idea that authorship would ever be totally my own. It gets closer to something I love about reading, what reading is like. The act of reading is always somewhat co-creative. I'm interested in how to make something like that, which is almost why the work is writing – the act of reading is done by whoever is performing the work. I'm not trying to abnegate authorial responsibility: I'm interested in acknowledging the necessary co-creativity of everything rather than destroying the sanctity of the authorial position. I'm not trying to destroy myself, I'm trying to acknowledge that everything is made with other people. The fact that I know it's

* Ian White was someone very important to me, both personally and for my work; 'what there is to be jubilant about is that limit is everyone's material and it is always here. And this is where to start': Ian White, 'F R E E (Prisons 2)', *Lives of Performers* blog, 29 October 2012, https://livesofperformers.wordpress.com/2012/10/29/f-r-e-e-prisons-2/.

made that way is because I did other jobs before. Any efficient machine puts everyone in their compartmentalised places and everyone is alienated. I'm trying to de-alienate this – it's not about the destruction of authorship.

There's an emptiness here. If I'd been here to see the space at Abteiberg, I'd have thought I needed to fill it with . . . I don't know, but I wouldn't have been able to hold the emptiness as it is. It's interesting, because I have made shows before that have used emptiness. But emptiness for a specific reason. When I've done things before that were empty, I realised afterwards that it was not a neutral thing to do. The removal was about power and it was violent. I was really giving more room to something else. My methodology is to feel the responsibility of what happens if you remove. What are you adding? What are you stating in that? What is your position in that? It isn't just a removal, you are placing your subjectivity in there, and your mess in there. I think if I'd been here, if I'd been able to encounter the space more fully, I probably would have filled it, because it would have made me nervous. I think I'm by nature, a filler; if there's a silence, I will fill it, you know. But I'm amazed now. And it shows that leaving a space empty doesn't need to be a process of aggressive removal, but can be left with life, life that is already happening. I think I feel it every time I do an exhibition, and every time I visit an exhibition, because I am sensitised to what's there from being an artist. I feel the sets of relationships, I feel them through the show. You see one show an artist did in a certain way, or another made in another way, and you can feel the joy, the pain, you can feel everything that happens in that space. It reminds you there is another way.

It's always historical, it's always material. We're always dealing with the context. There's no degree of deconstruction, in that there is no zero-point of void, it doesn't exist, because it's always within something, it's always in the mess of life. There's an abstract notion of deconstruction to a clean or evacuated point; actually what making a space brings you down to is not absence, but the presence of life. It brings you down to the dirt, to the trauma of living conditions, the conditions that are always here but that we don't always acknowledge.

I come from a structural film background, which is the knowledge of what your means of production are. Working with your means of production, acknowledging the structures and materials of production, and using those limits in some way as material. I use the analogy of what happens in cinema when you go beyond the ninety-minute mark, there's a reaction: Oh, but this doesn't fulfil the criteria! And somehow this exhibition is similar. It doesn't fulfil my internalised criteria of 'exhibition'. I am presented with the same materials, but used in a different way. That plasticity is important to me.

Using the score and not being in the space during the install has produced something else. To see it wrought on this scale, it's really mind-bending, it's fabricated a new scenario of what a show can be for me. It's in part to do with the space itself. But also the limitations, because what I had to work with, ultimately, was limitations, including emotional ones, and I finally worked with that material to produce something else. That's what I'm always trying to do in the work. I have an insecurity about what my labour form is, because it's so imprecise, and so uncontracted: I have this weird thing where I feel like I should be doing more work constantly. There's this feeling like, I'm not working enough – because you can't validate the type of work we do as artists. And so very often, I'll be working with something and I'll begin to overwork it out of a kind of anxiety. But I simply couldn't do that here. I think the score here has produced something that's gone way outside of my control. I think if the openness had been fashioned by me, then it would have been much more proprietary.

There's a specific moment I remember in the process. I'd been working with the floor plans, and the museum is very complex and open and has a structure at play that is very loud in many ways, due to the architect Hans Hollein's postmodern design.

I was invited to show in the exhibition hall, which is the space for temporary exhibitions, but this is a place that was designed to have no walls: the space flows directly into the collections space and permanent works are on display in the exhibition hall. And at first in my process I tried to box things in. I wanted to cover the Lawrence Weiner. I wanted to cover all the permanent works in the exhibition hall. Blank it out. I wanted to build loads of walls, I wanted to block out the other works. I was trying to get *my* space. Then at a certain point I noticed my own conservatism in this, my own prejudices. Then slowly I realised I could just try to flip things – this limit, this problem, could be the very vulnerability and material I work with in this case. Flood it! Make everything porous, let it go everywhere! What happens if you just pour water in? All the seams will go, it will just flood. Just let that be, you know. There isn't a precise border. Yet, bizarrely, it's made entirely of borders.

I think as well in my own life I've been trying to compartmentalise what I was, as a mother, as an artist . . . Because when you can compartmentalise, you can understand a thing, and you can make it efficient and you can profit from it. There is a need to segregate yourself into parts in order to profit, to be successful in one part at the cost of all the others. When you don't compartmentalise, it's all porous. I find that intimidating. I had to sit with the complete porosity of everything, and then, within that, create boundaries that allow different things to breathe and allow the identity of two different things to exist. Compartmentalising is not that, it's enclosure so you can understand the metrics of the parts, it's like a performance that the other parts do not exist. What happens if you embrace problems? What happens if you understand your complicity in issues? How can I understand my space in that building without removing other people's work? It is not the Lawrence Weiner that is blocking me, it's what I understand subjectively as 'Lawrence Weiner' that is blocking me. When I managed to abandon this conservative modus operandi it got more interesting and far more critical, because I stopped trying to keep a place in the system I thought I should be in.

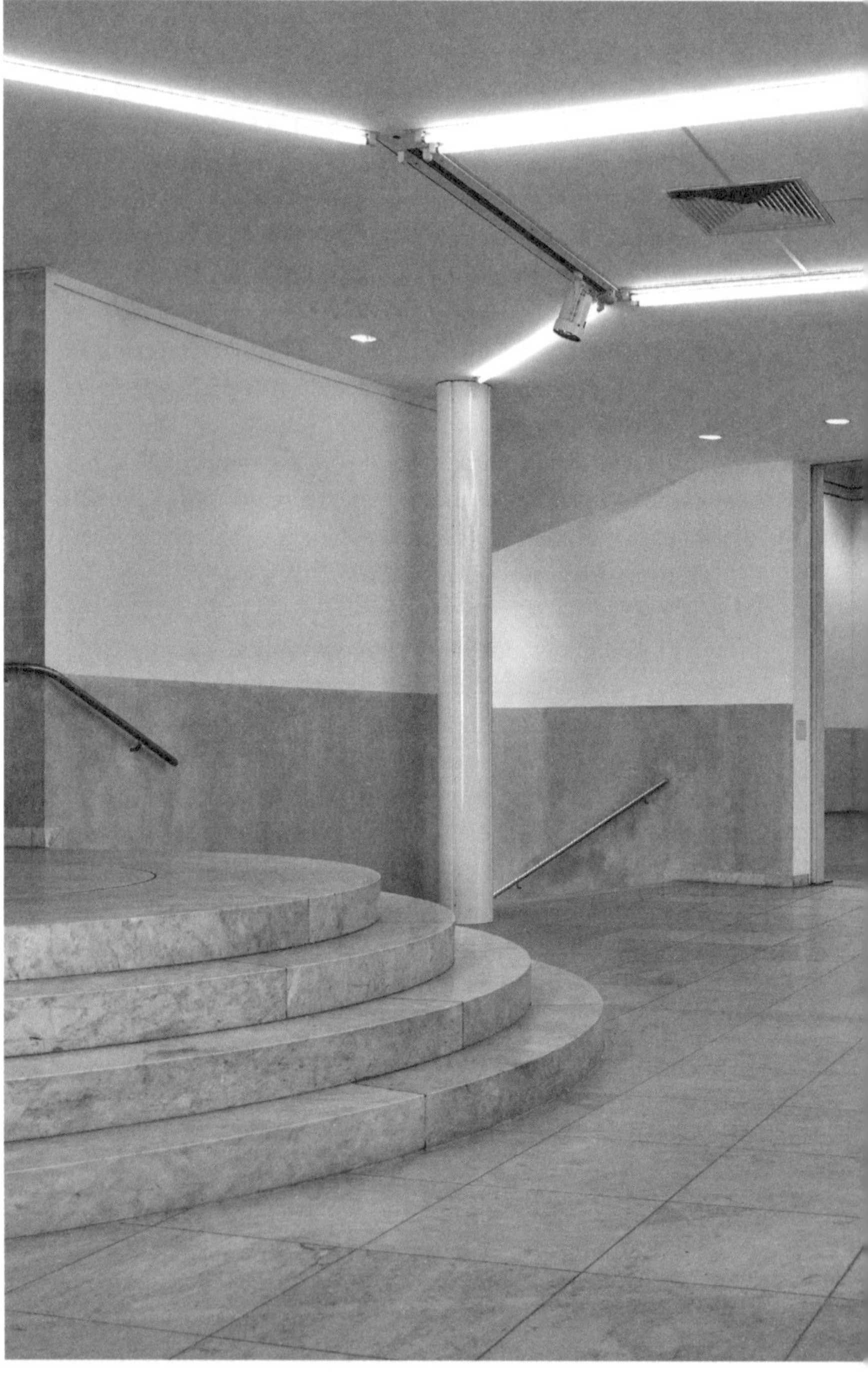

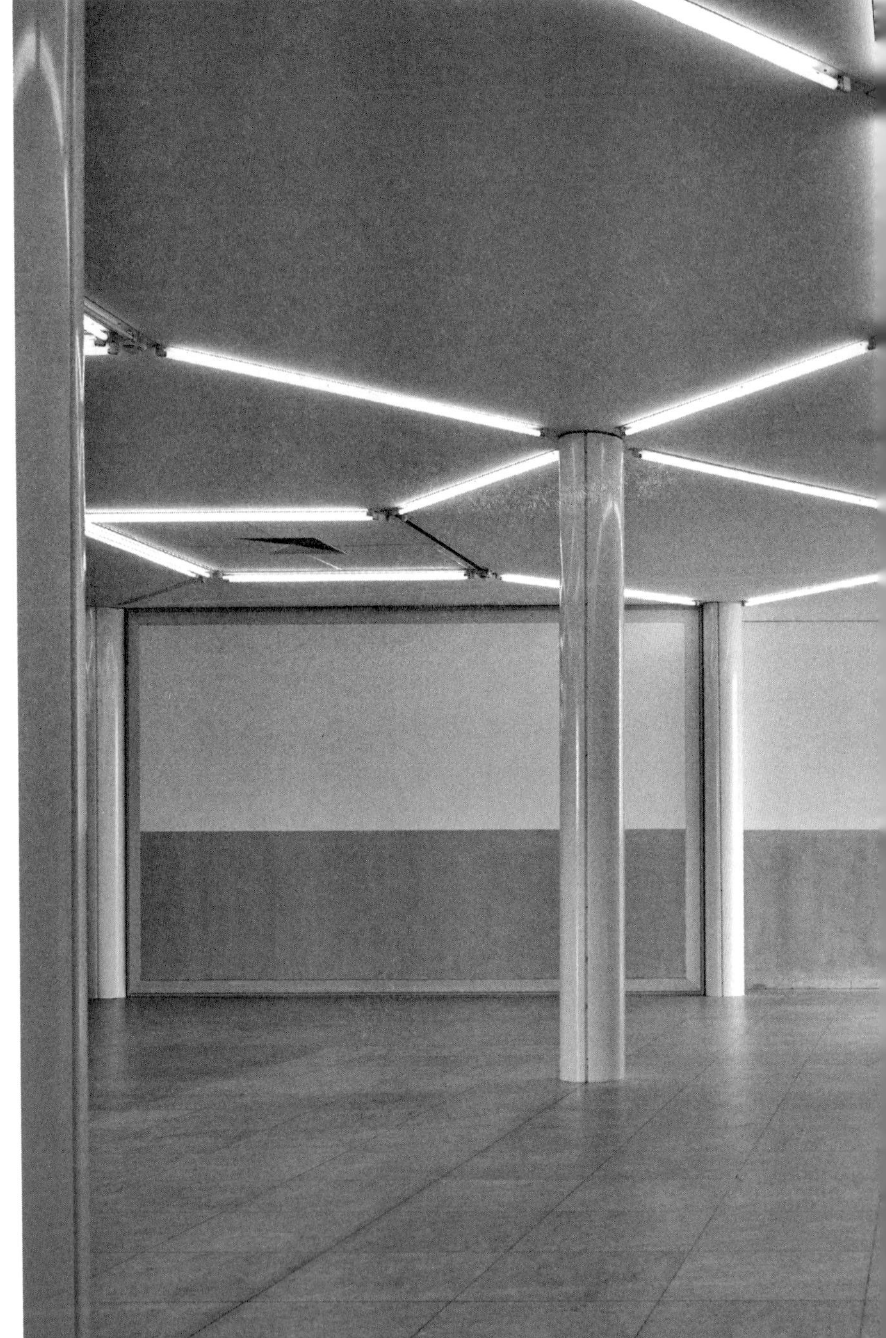

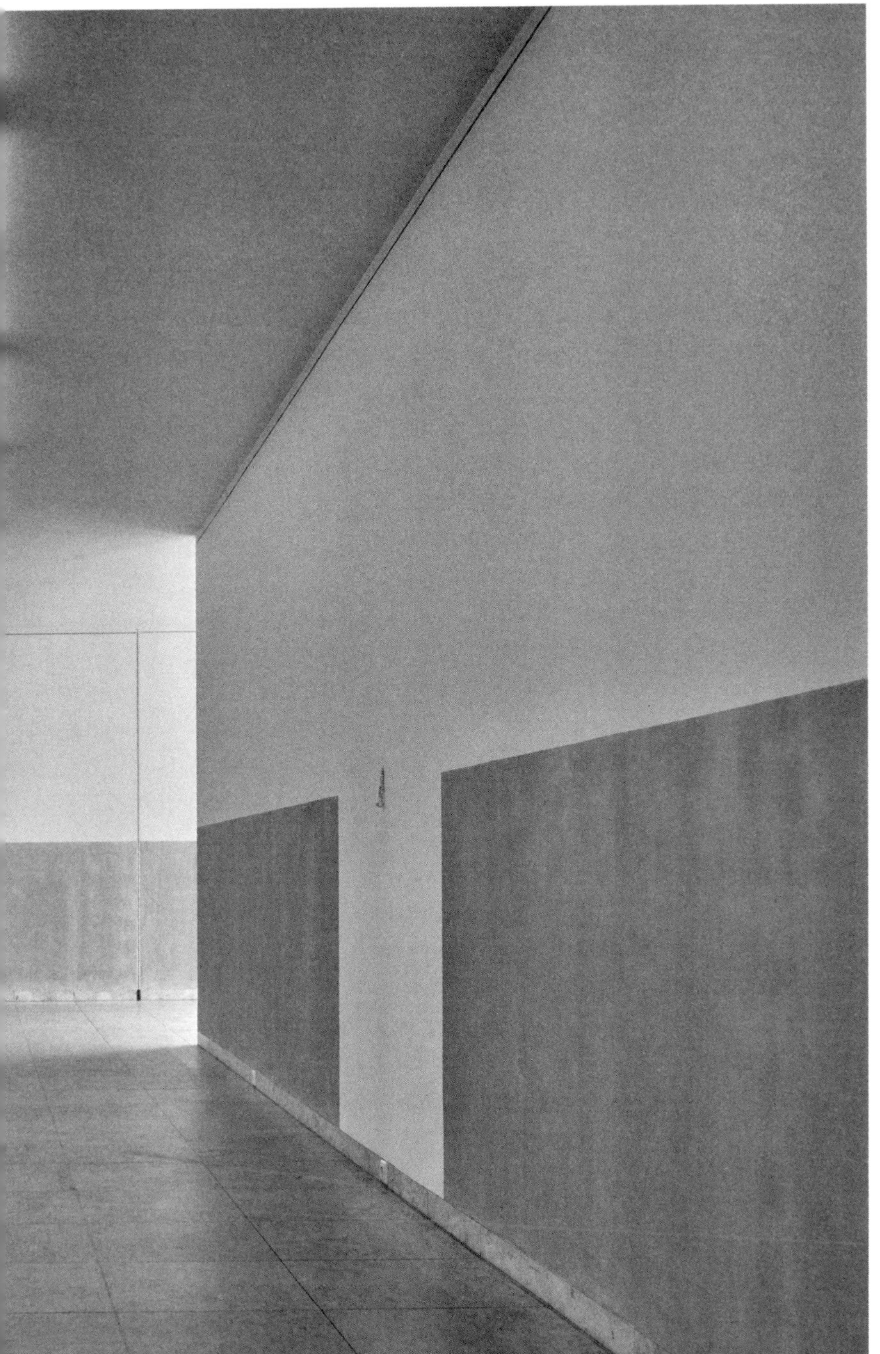

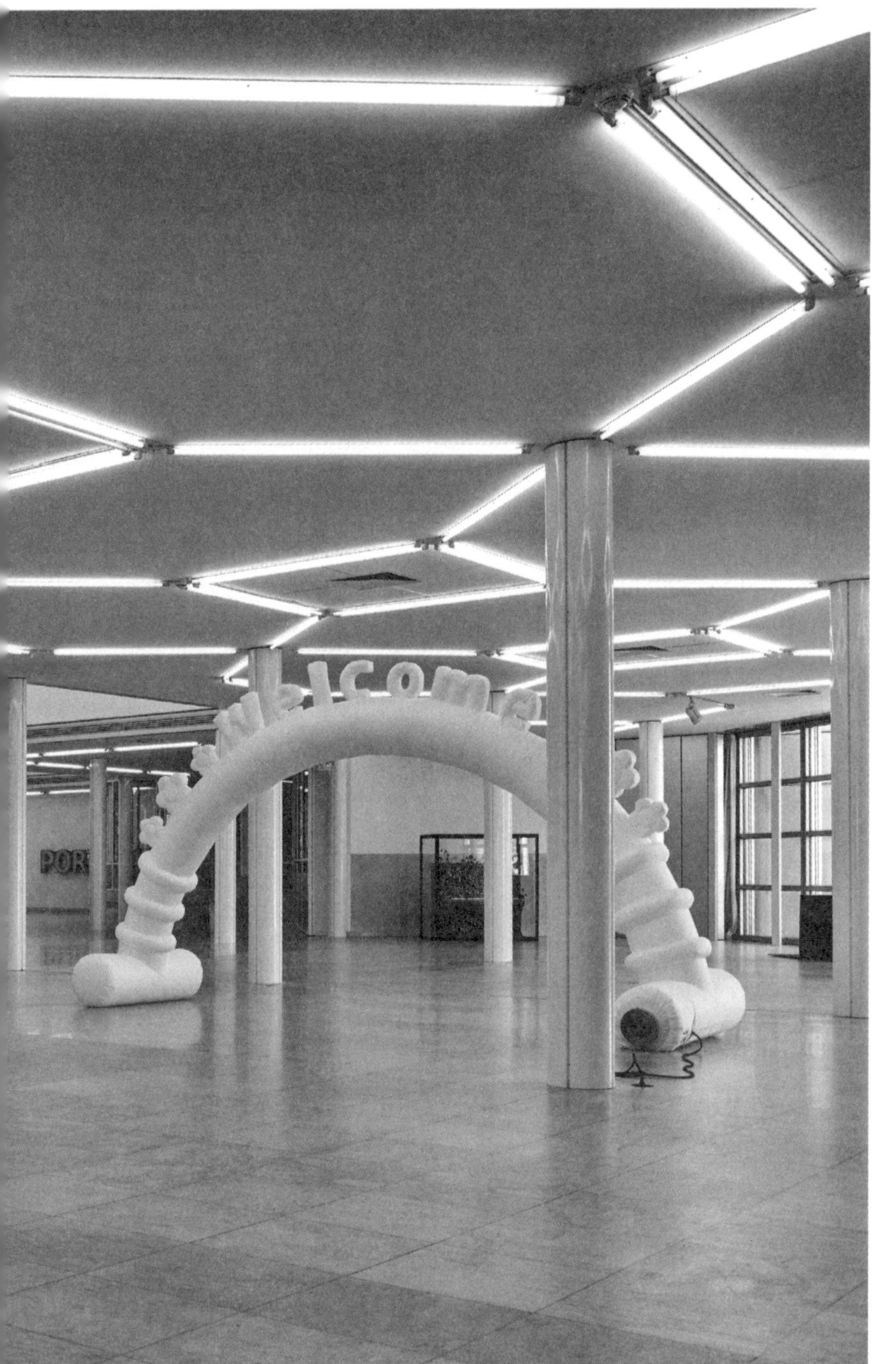

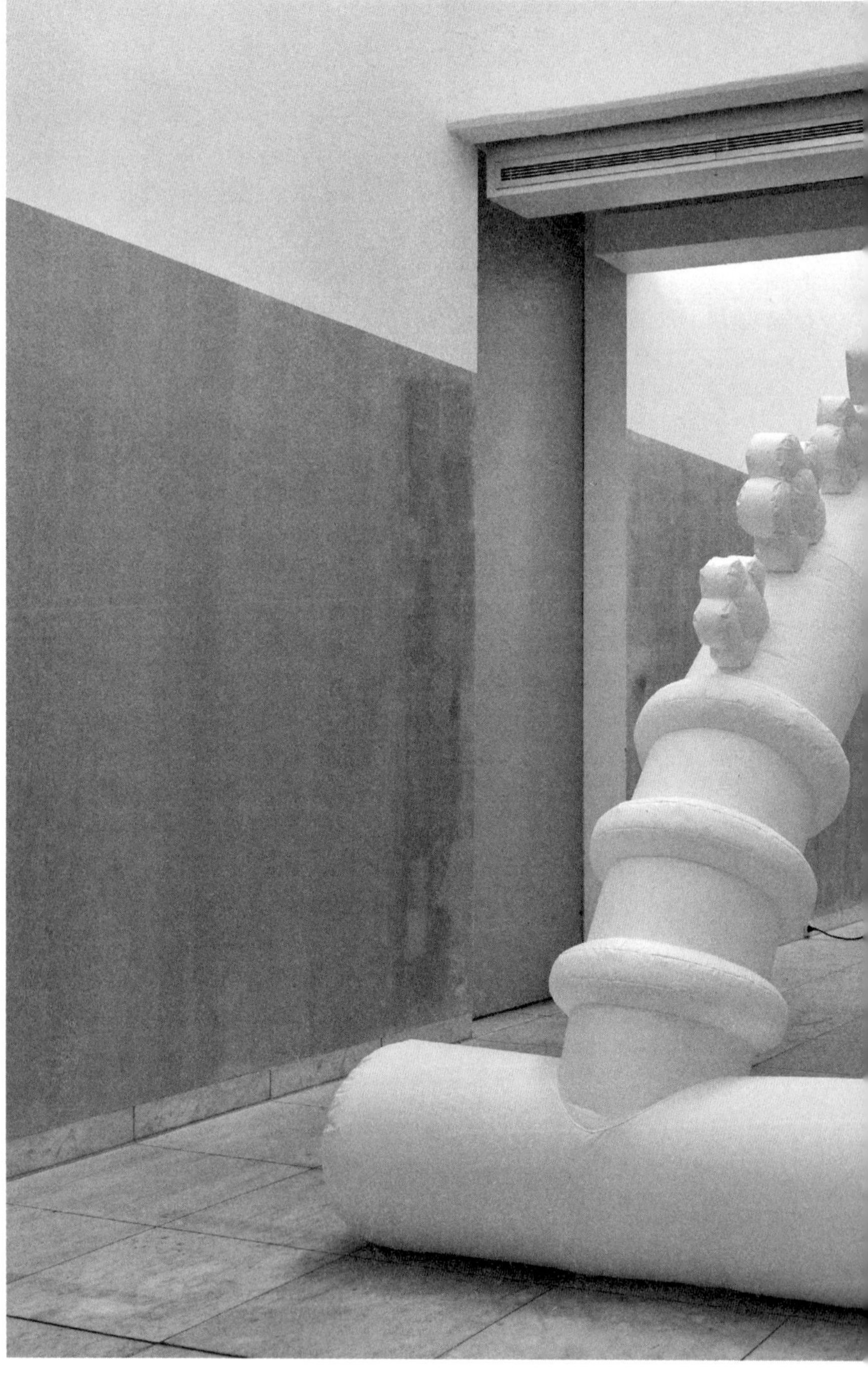

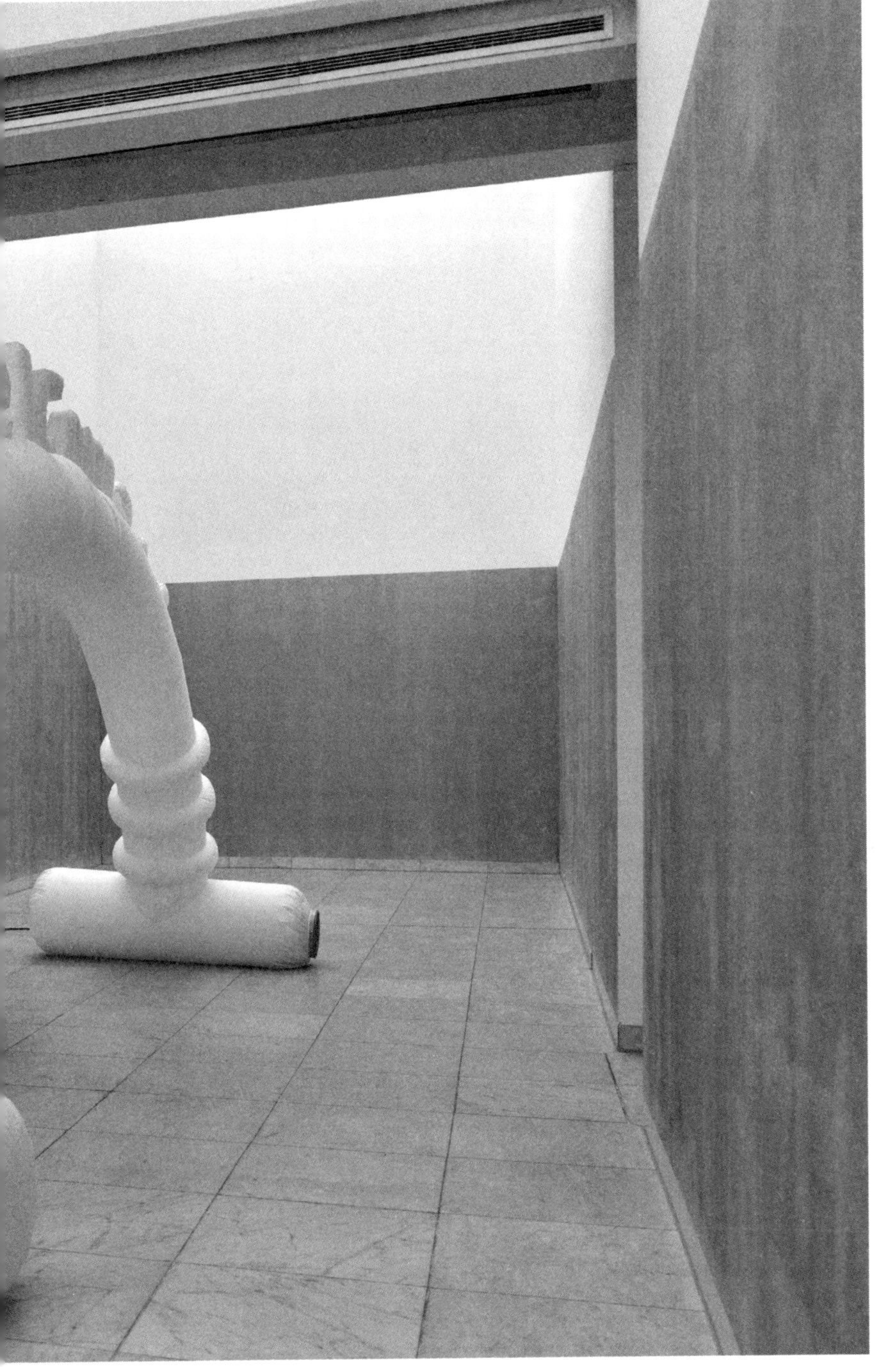

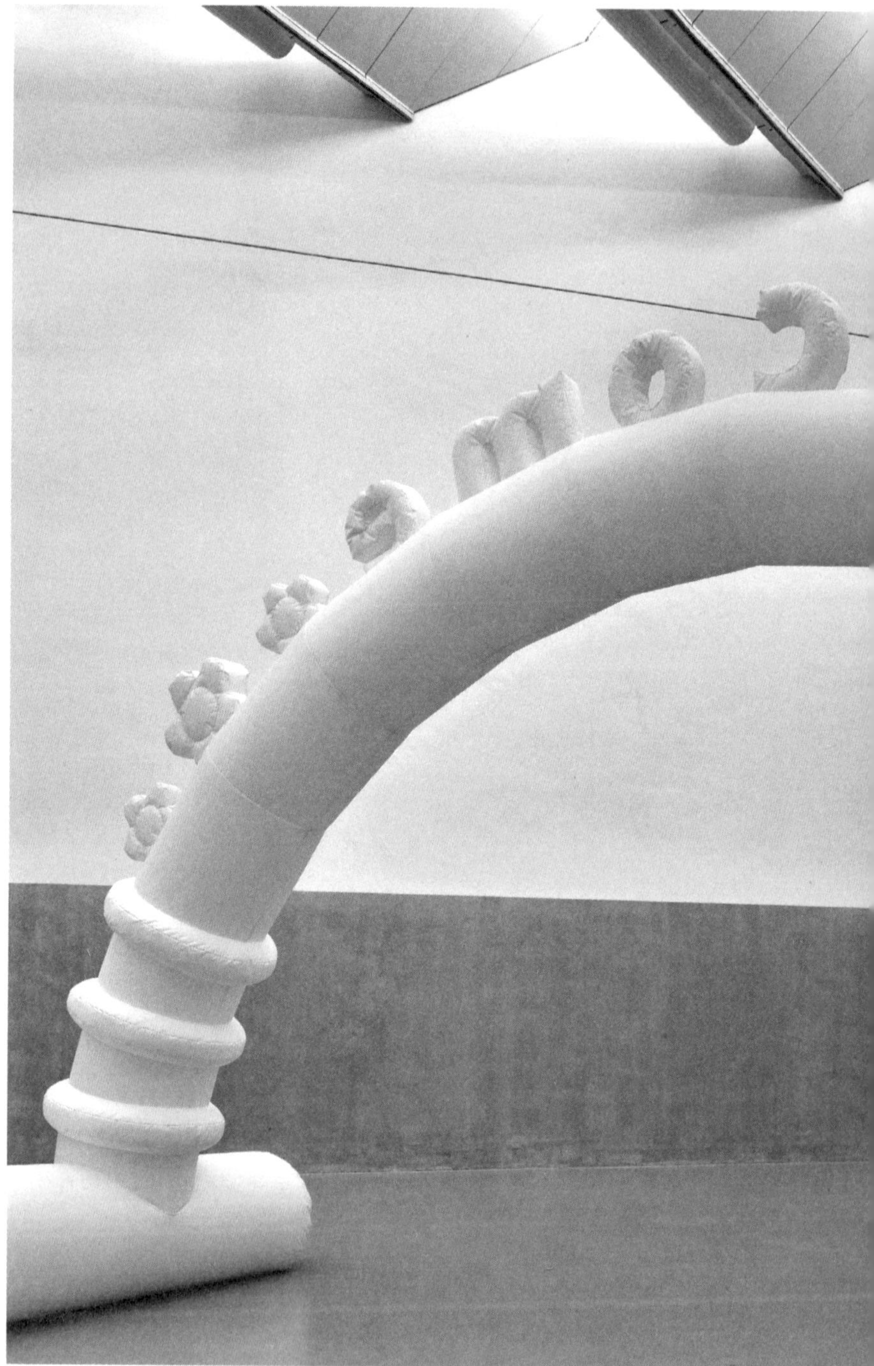

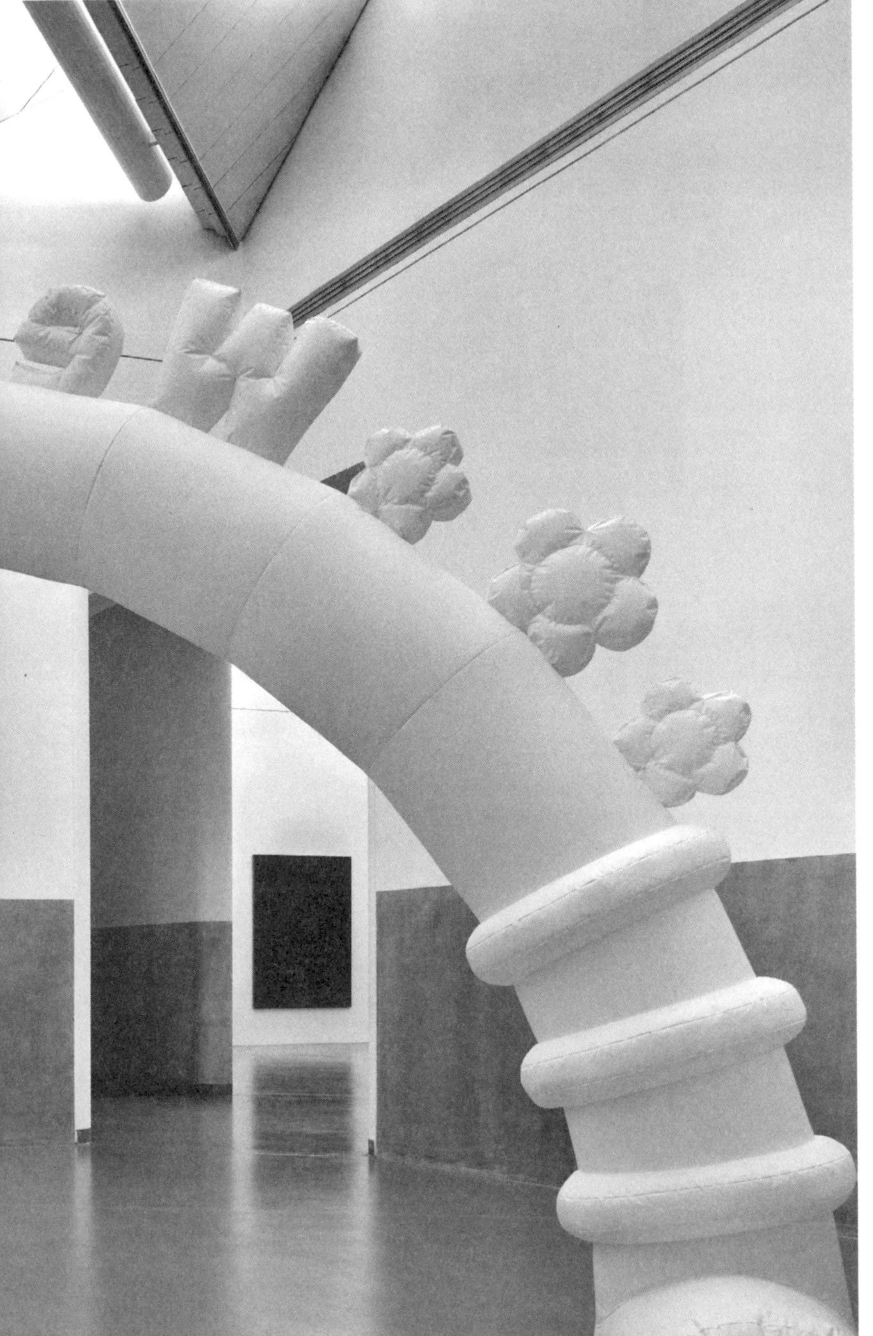

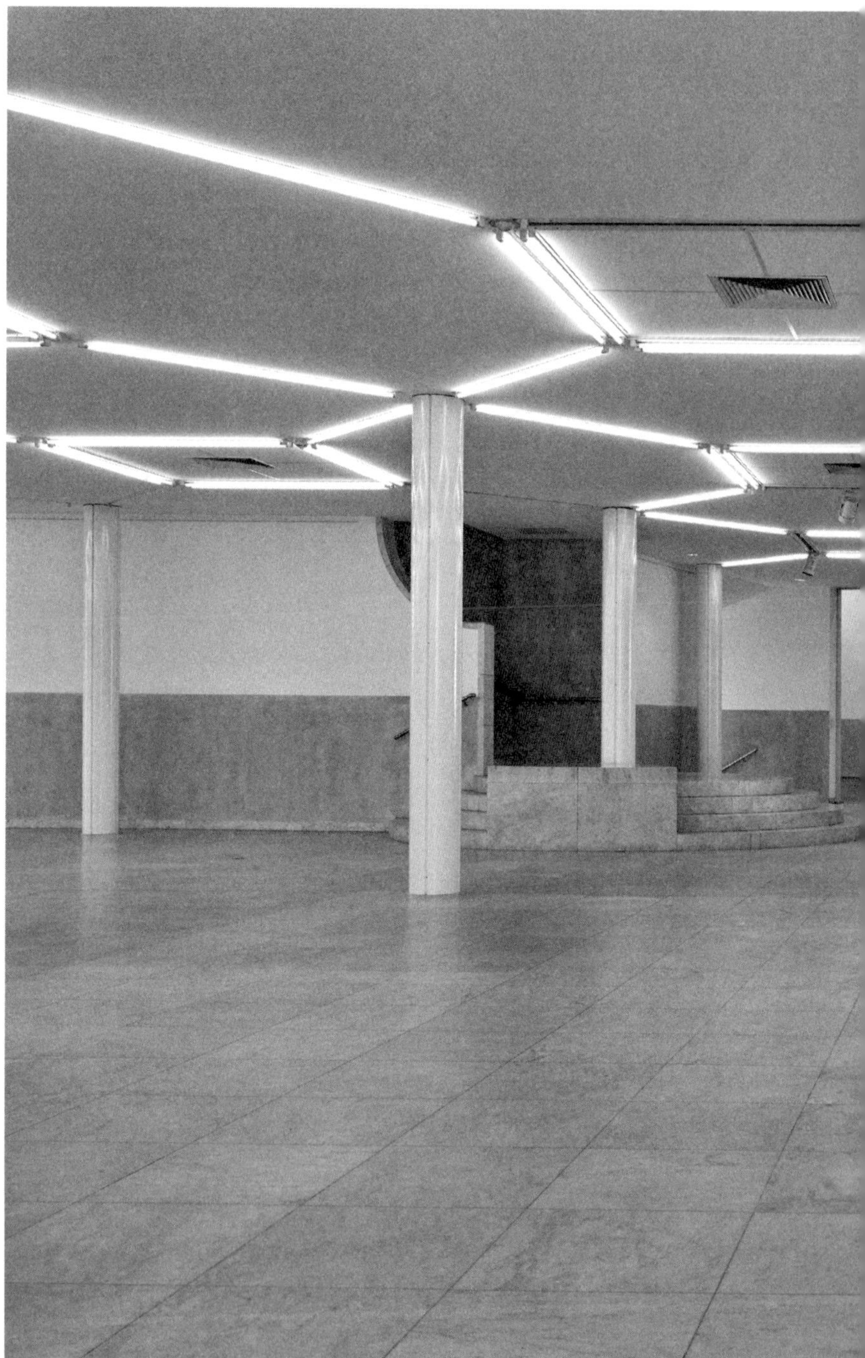

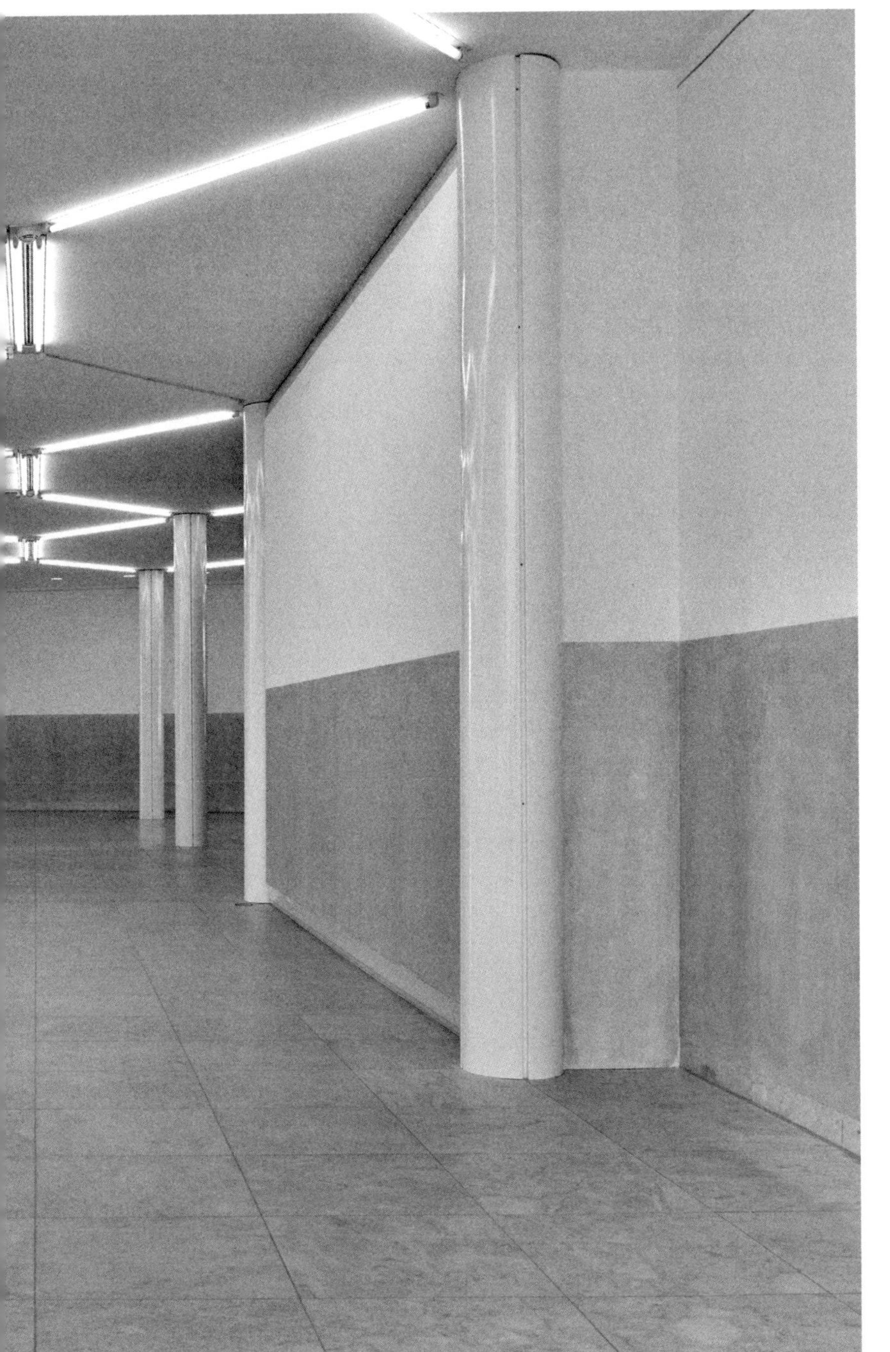

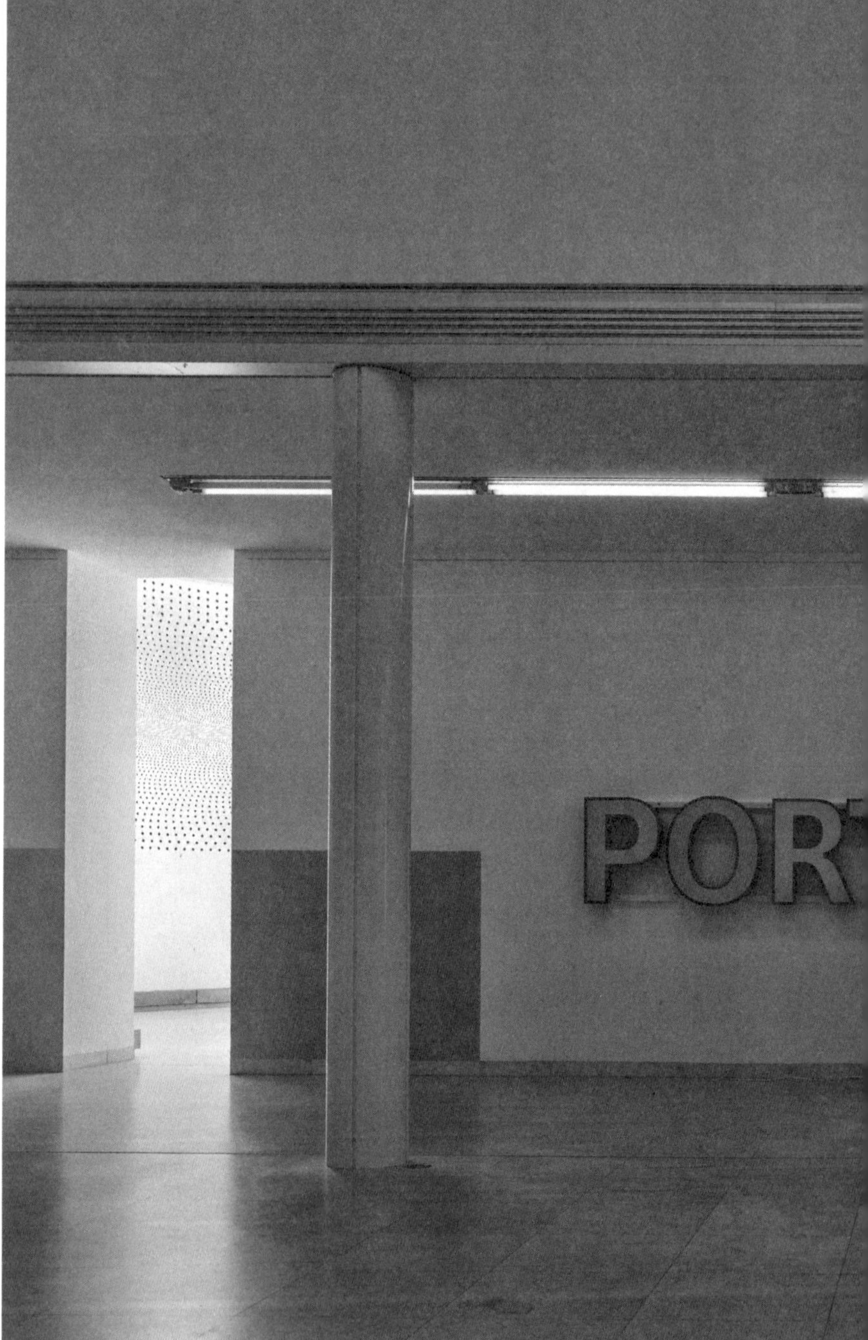
POR

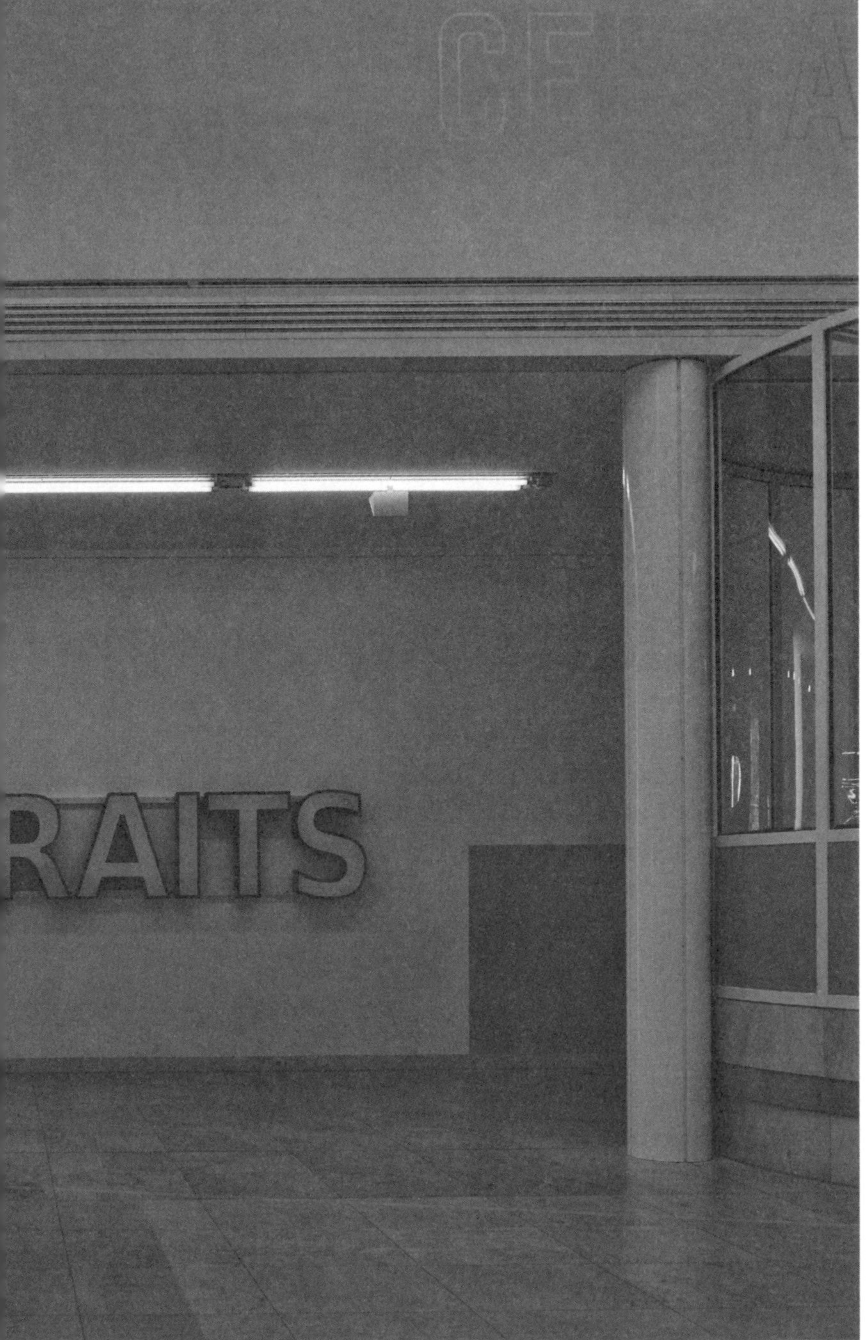
RAITS

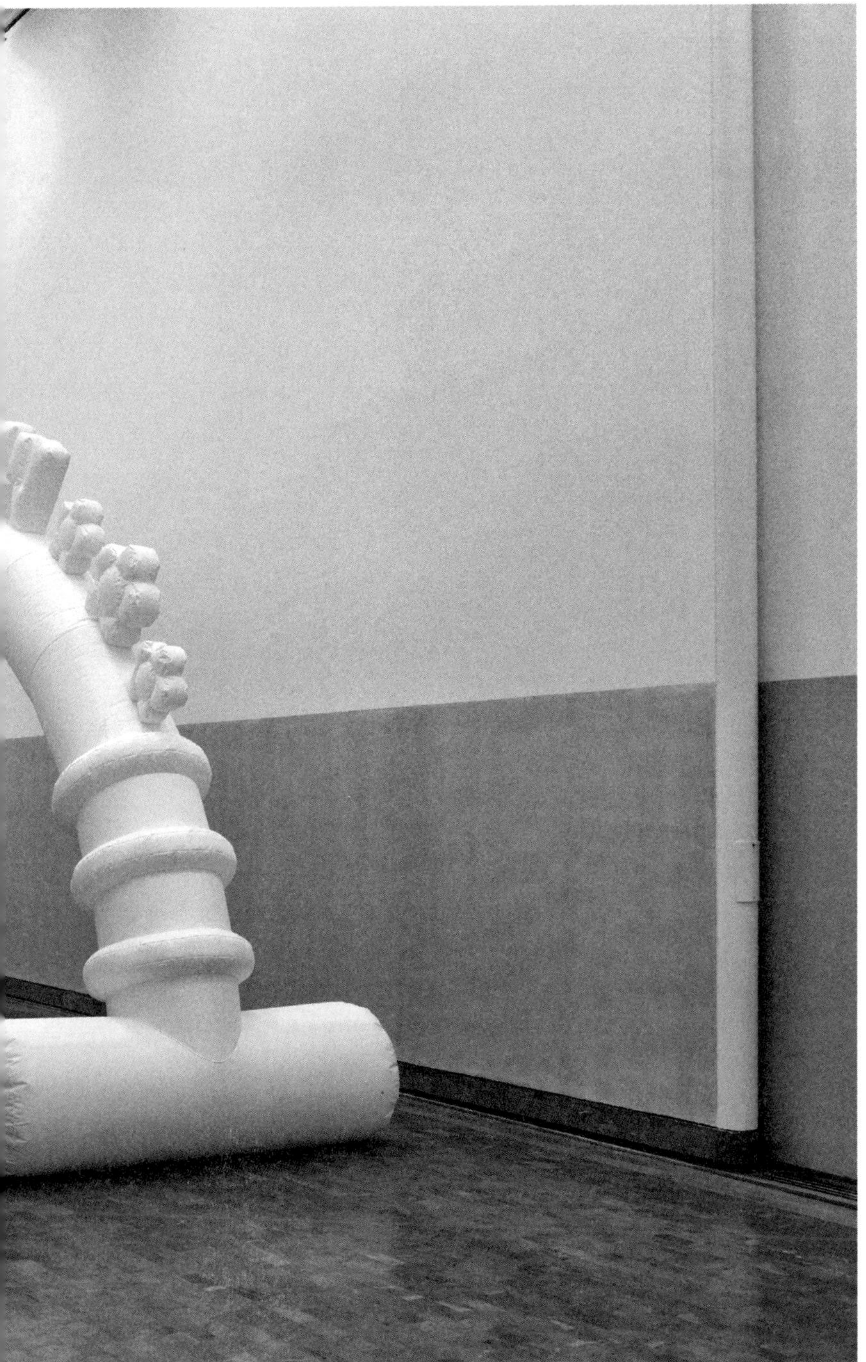

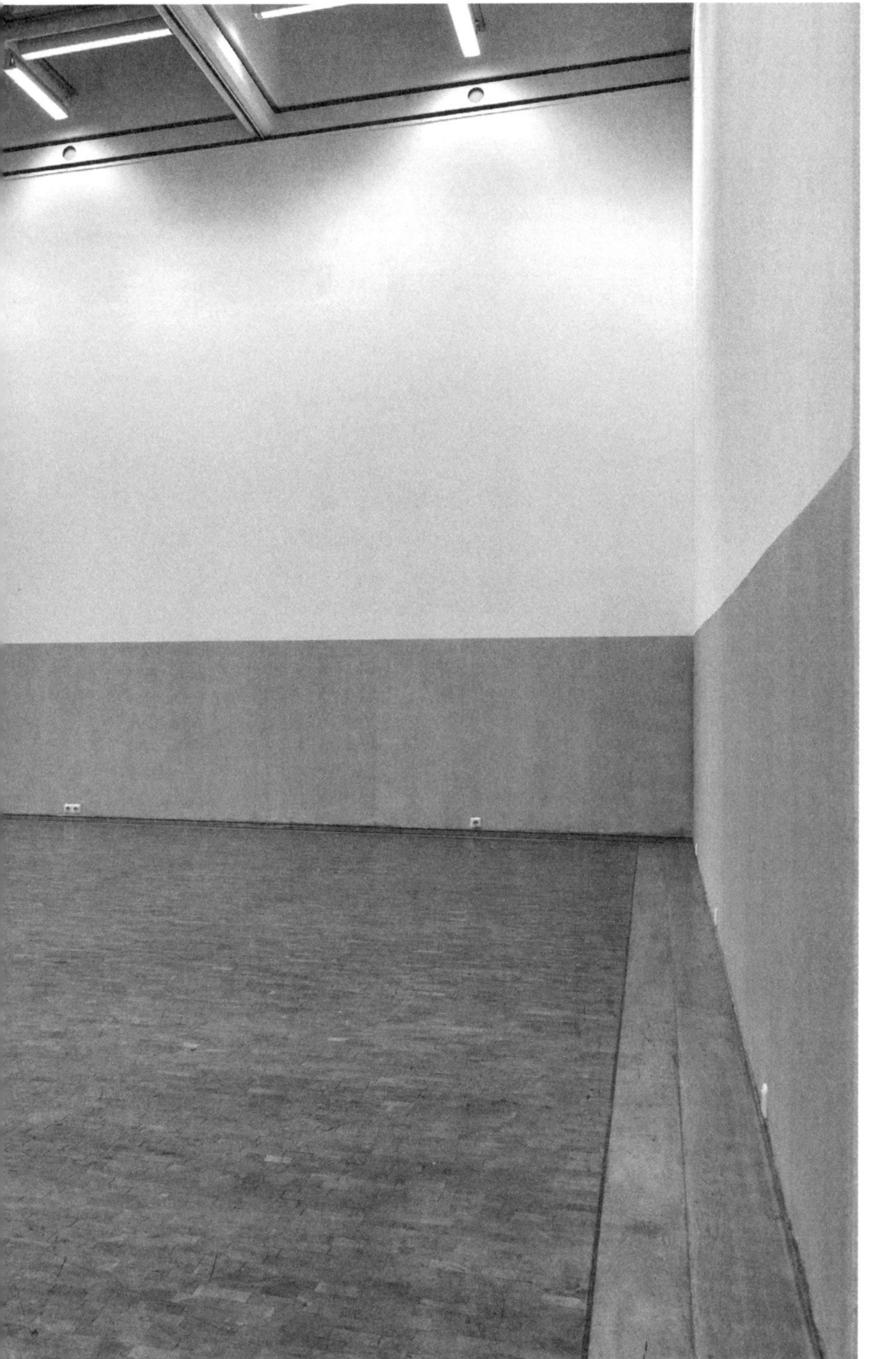

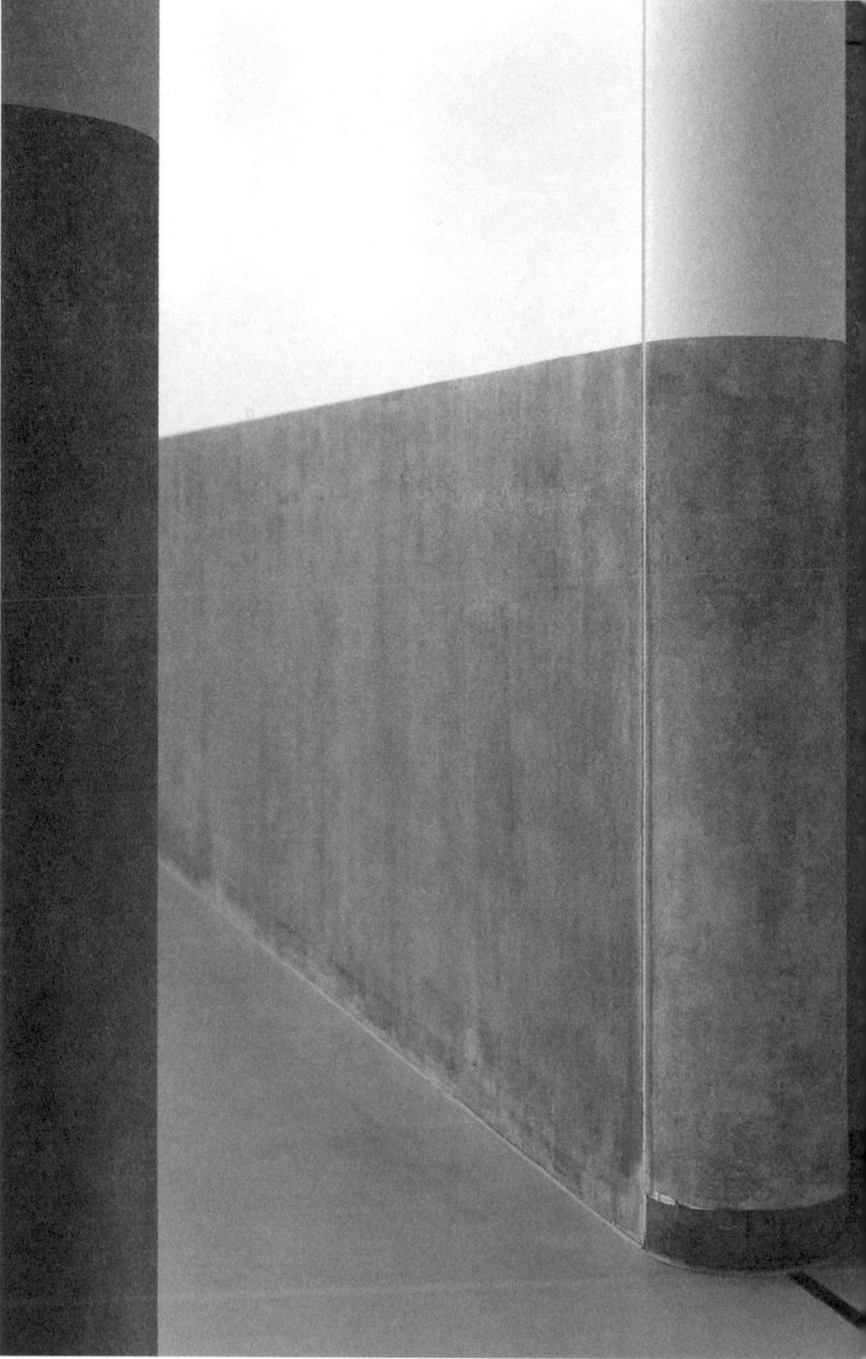

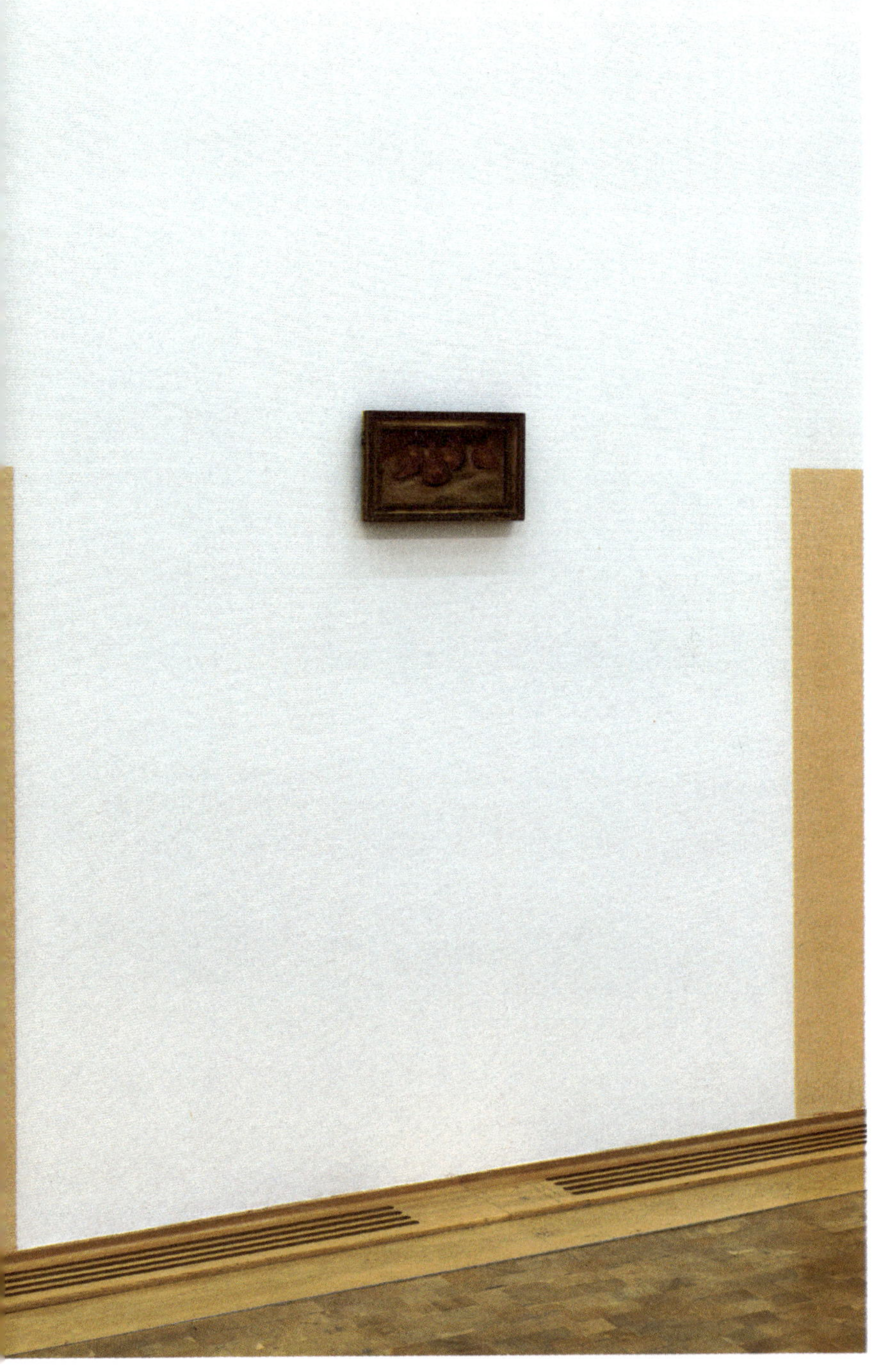

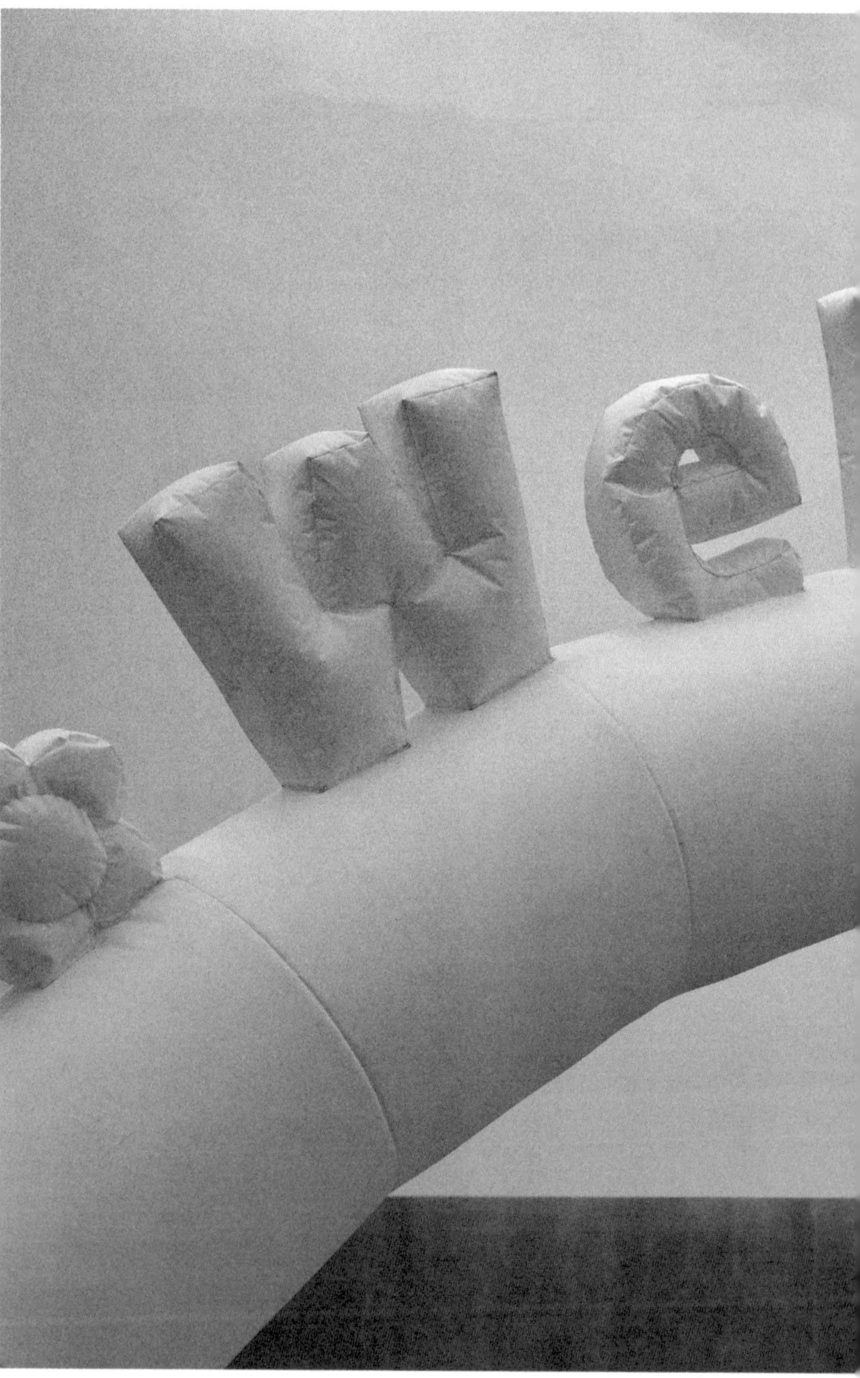

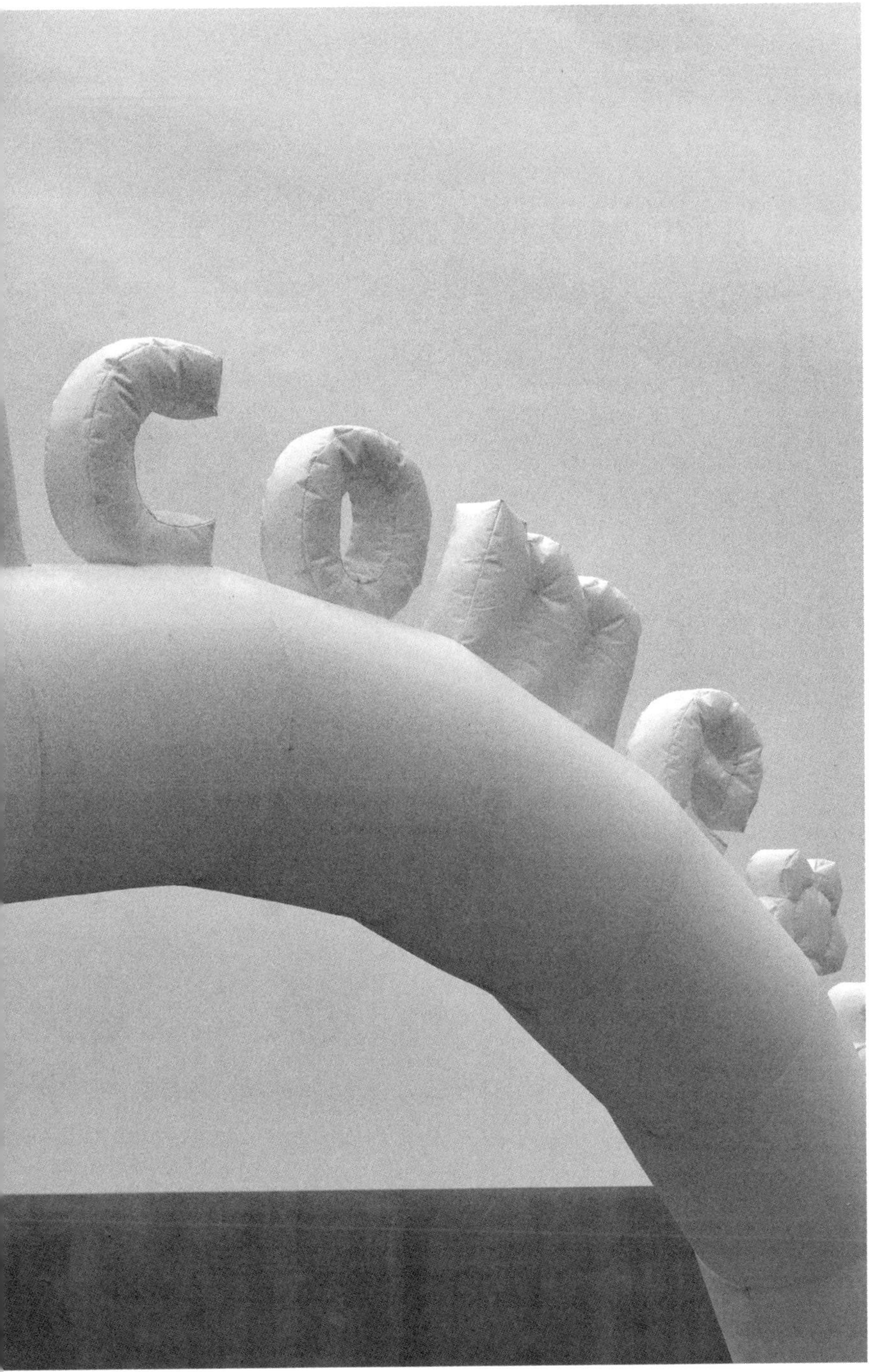

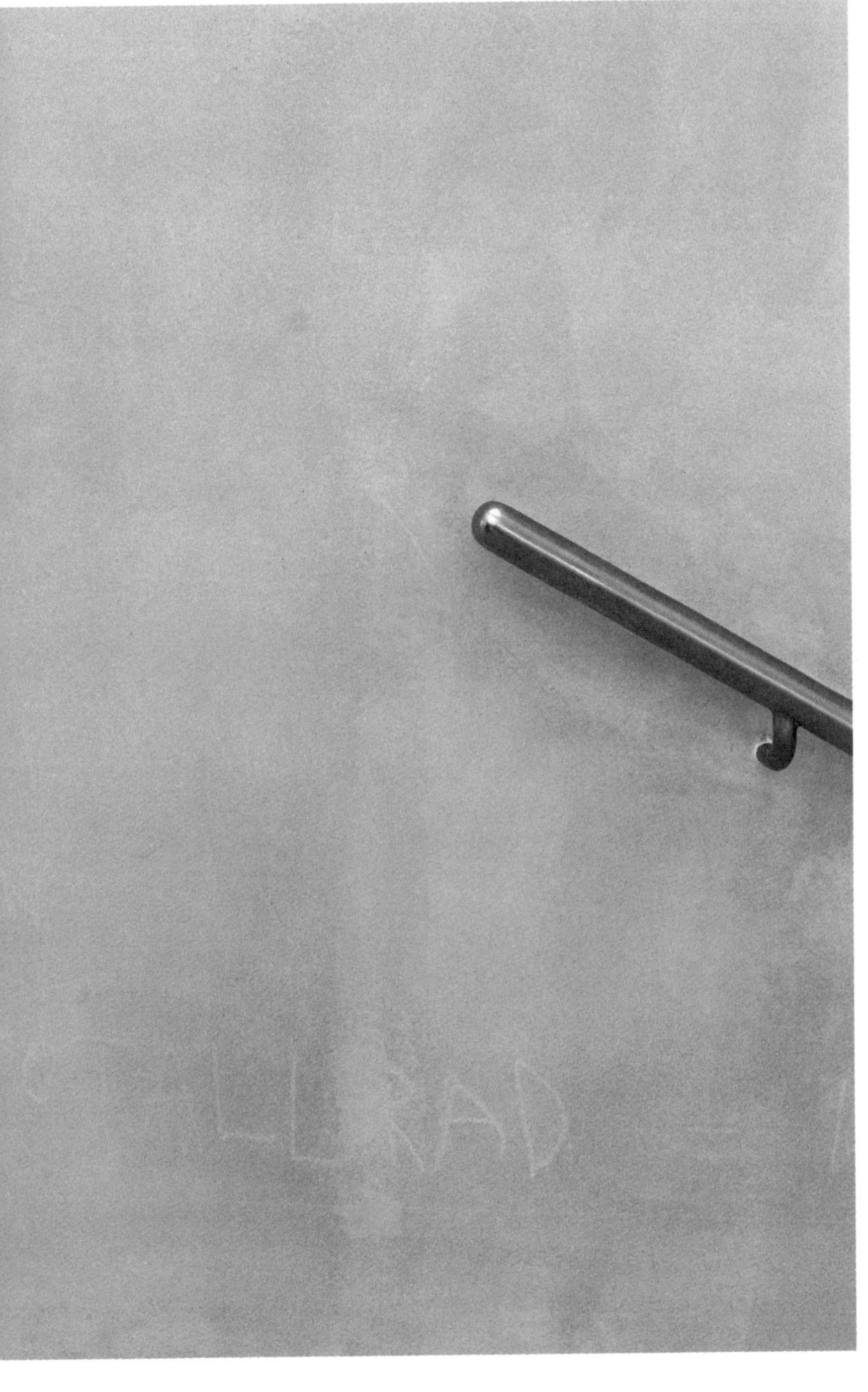

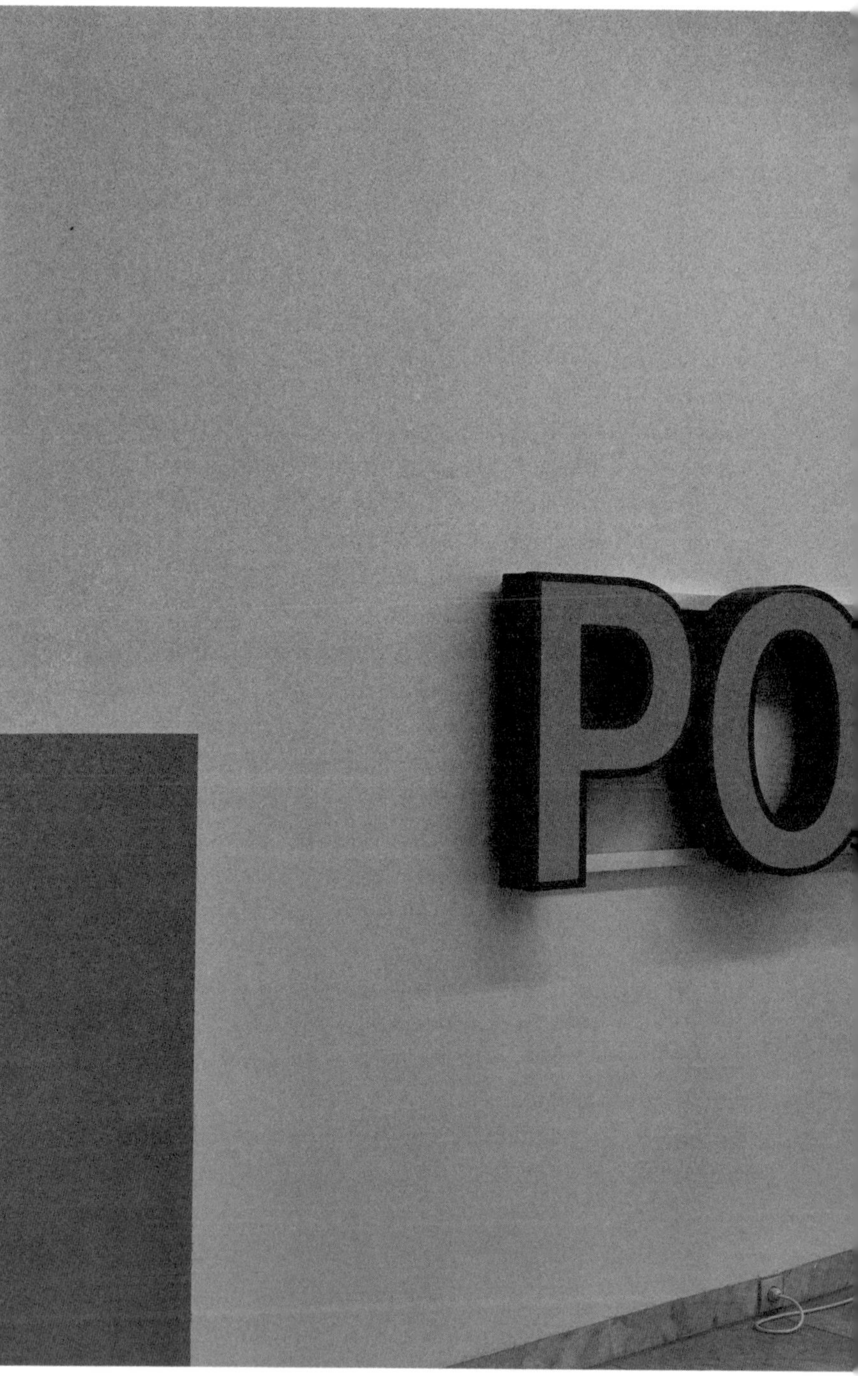
PO

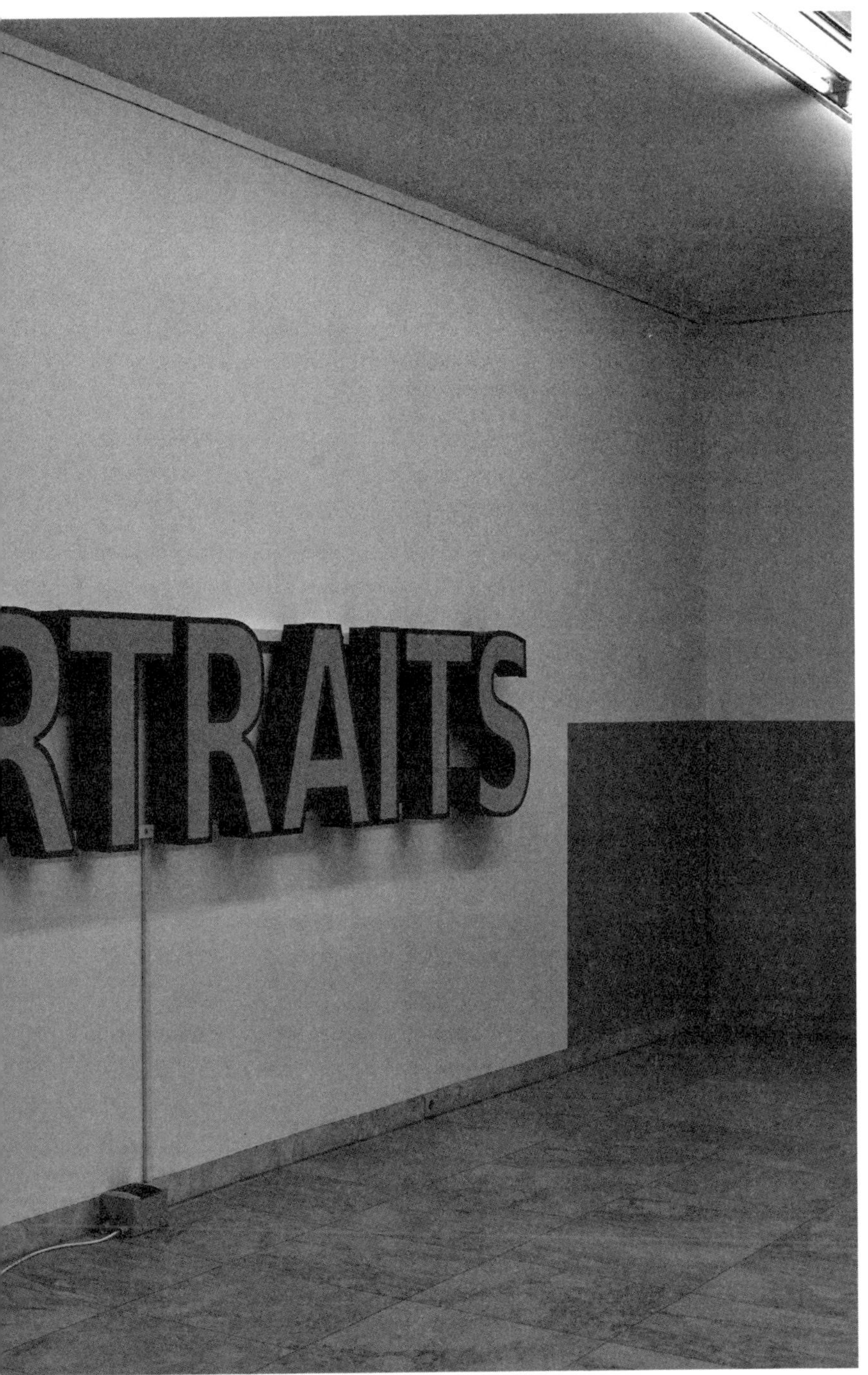
RTRAITS

BLOW
CERTA
RTRAITS

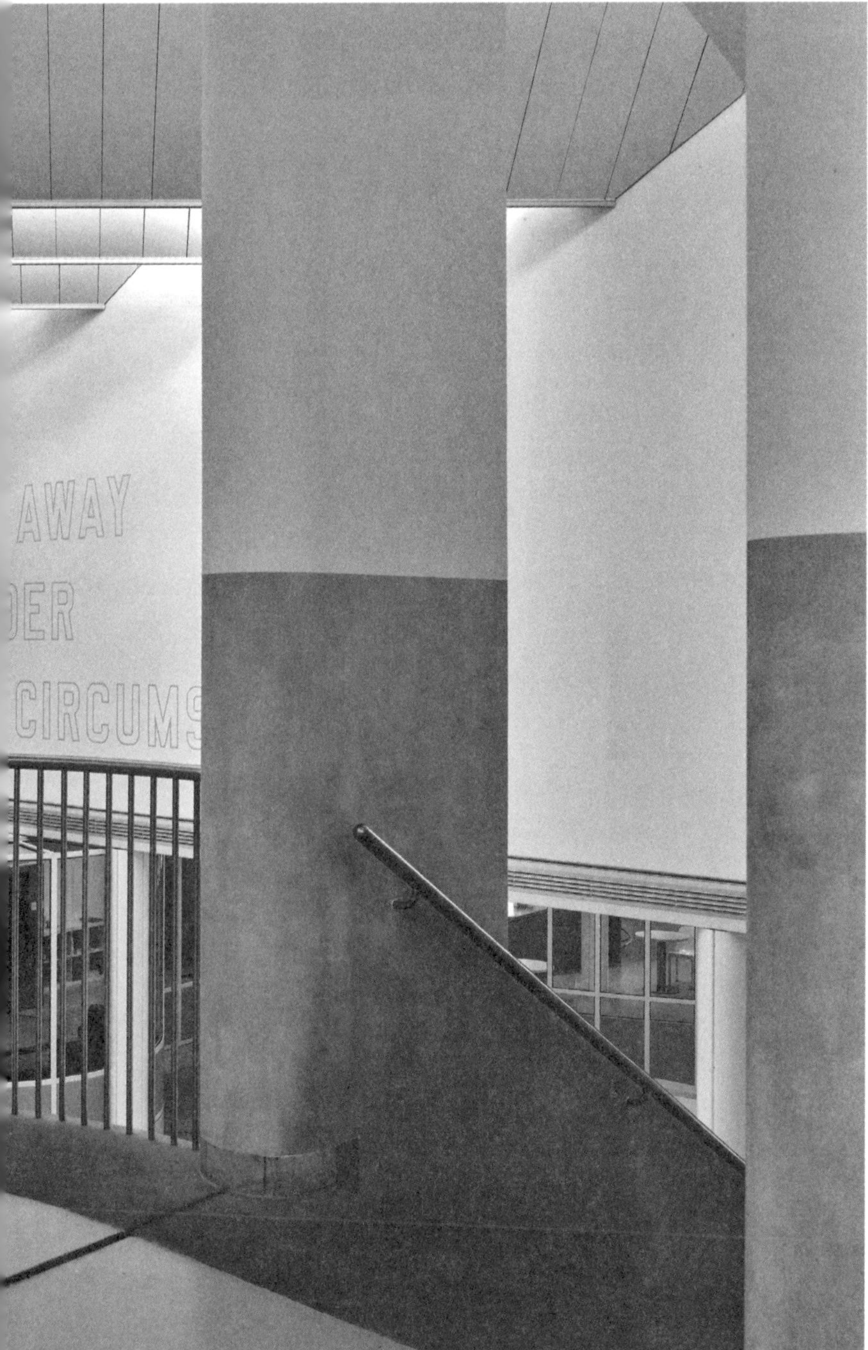

AWAY
DER
CIRCUMS

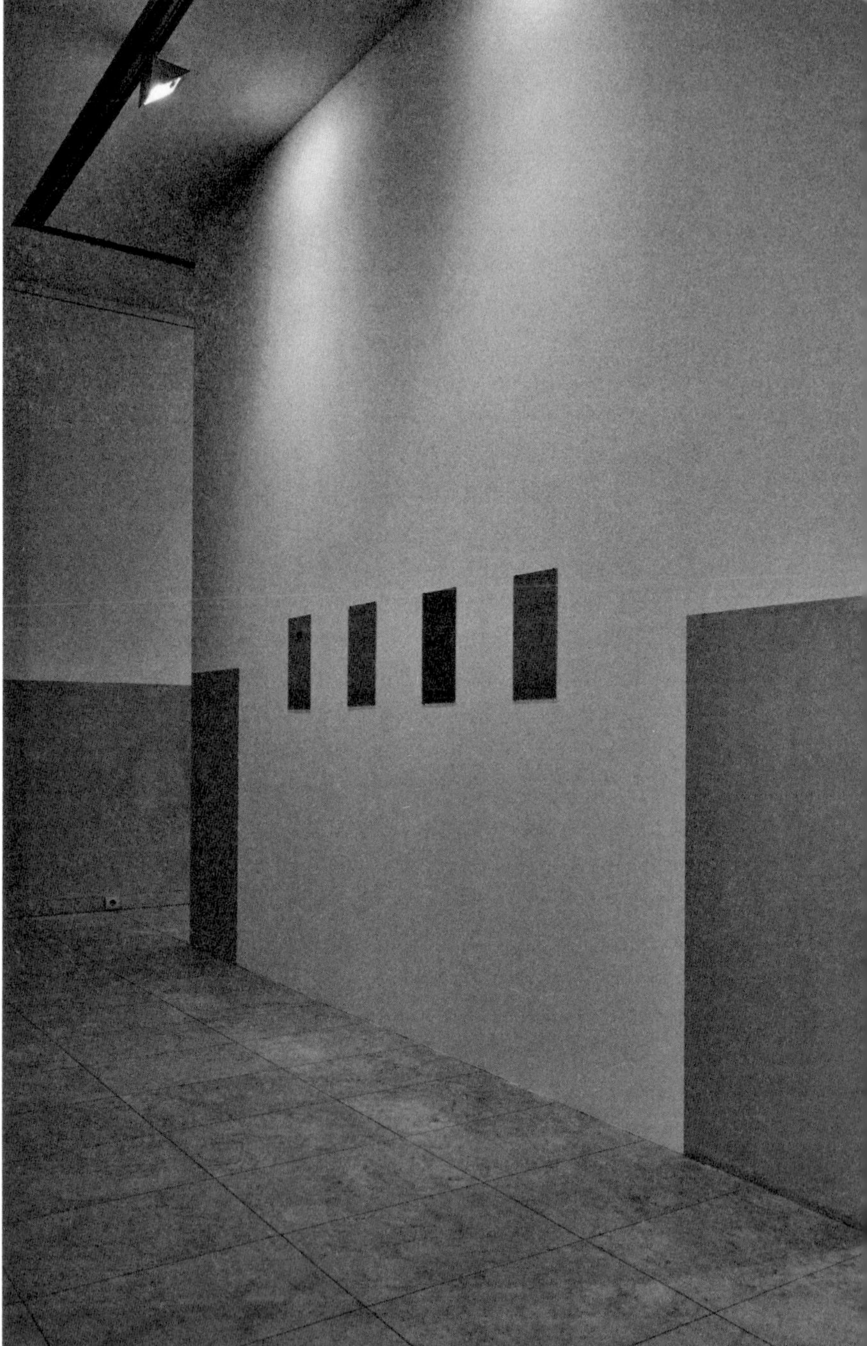

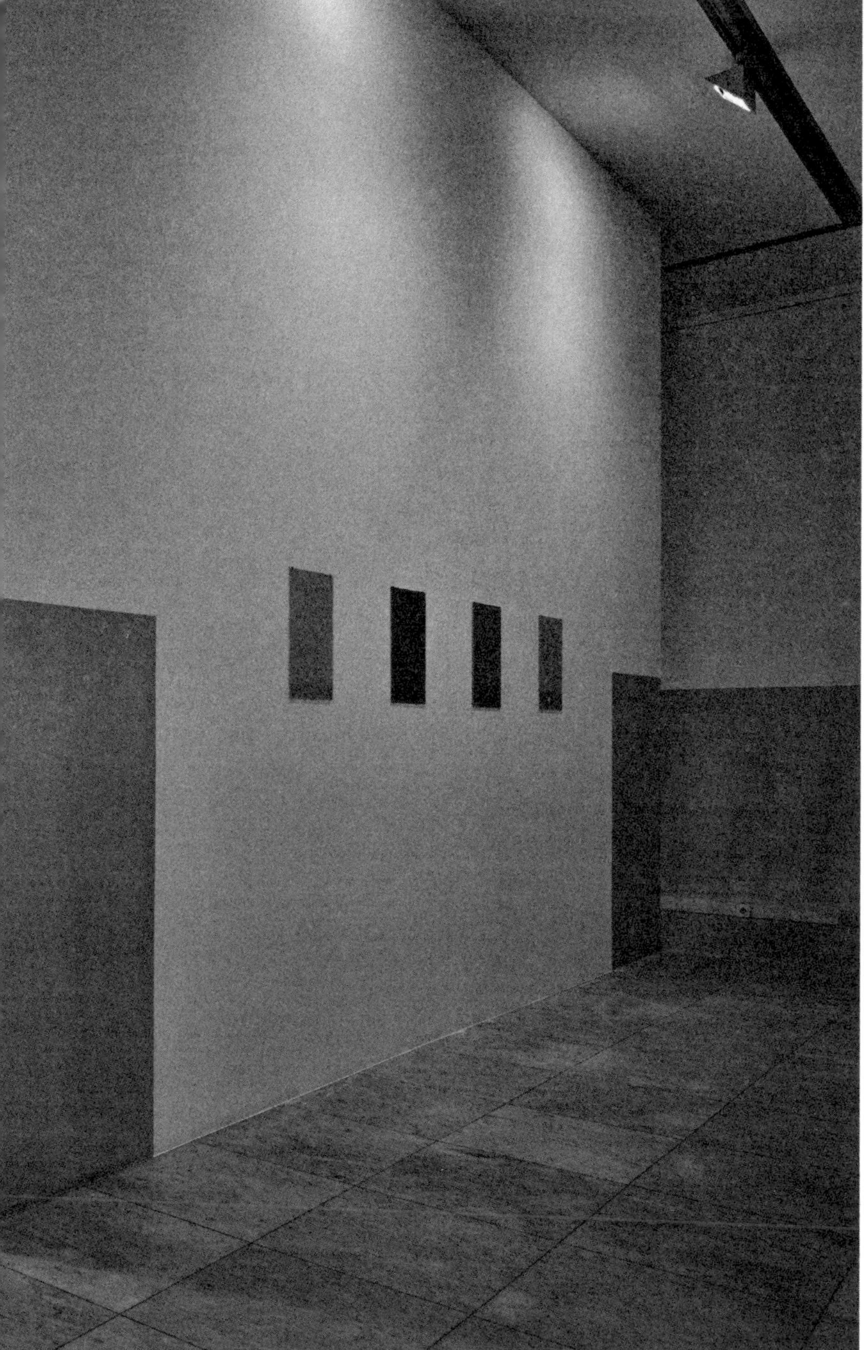

Browns is the flood for me. It is the work where the walls are painted with brown paint to hanging height, on all available walls. 'Available' is where it got interesting, because volumes and spaces are included that are not always deemed as good space, space good for art. What I love about *Browns* actually, is that because of the very thin, watery quality of the paint, the brown is not actually about brownness, but about whiteness, about the construction of whiteness. Brown is a vehicle to show the maintenance of this whiteness, including the scratched paintwork hidden by white, including the labour, the good walls, the bad walls. *Browns* showed all of that in its thinness. I initially proposed a sort of shiny brown latex paint, and I think the realisation actually came from, again, a limitation: Susanne and I were talking about how it would leave a line when it was painted over because of the thickness of the paint. This has produced something else that is in excess of what I could visualise. The brown walls fill this institution, where the invisibility of white walls is constantly maintained.

As an artist, I have done the bit at the end of the install where I mop the floors, touch up the walls, and try to maintain that constructed whiteness-form, and the effortless neutrality of the space. The more involved you get in working with museums, in their programmes, the more insulated the construction of white space is: electrical sockets fully hidden in the ceiling etc. I think it's interesting how frightened we are, I am, of the collapse of that construct.

What surprises me, and why this feels different from shows I've made in the past, which have a similar movement of removal because of what happens when you begin to question the construct, is that it's traumatic, and it's also love, and mess, and life; but it's loss too. We are institutionalised. I am part of it, so the collapse of it is felt as a loss, and then it's the opening of love, and that's where humanity is. It's not in the perfection of anything. I think that when you're open to that – inclusive of an acknowledgement of your own prejudices, or your own history, or your own complicity – it is real. We are tied to this bad funding stream, or this bad situation, but what begat that funding stream or this situation is this industry. The industry came first and is absolutely tied to the creation of what is problematic. I think the history of privilege has been about utilising those ties to extract, and then the cutting off those ties, to retain. I think what's important about acknowledging those ties and keeping them there is that there's suddenly porosity again, which leads to a flood of questions. And it's also the acknowledgement of community, the acknowledgement of other people and that you are dependent on each other. The works that are inflated archways, saying Welcome, called *Arches*, are very literally dependent on air and electricity, they are dependent on something and also someone actually coming into them. The ability to welcome or for an institution to be accessed is dependent on a host of factors, a lot of other things that have happened already.

Understanding my desire to cover up the Lawrence Weiner, for instance, is part of an understanding that what I do essentially depends, can only depend, on these histories. Even if I move away from them, they're still in relation to me. Rather than trying to attempt to erase or to evacuate everything, just letting all of that in. Think of the artist as an institution, as being inside and not in any outside position. You can't exclude anything, because you are part of it. There are two institutions crossing over, and one is myself. There are problems with both systems of regulations. That thing when you get into a bath that's the same temperature as you, or when the summer comes and you start wearing fewer clothes and the wind touches your skin, that's what I want. That's what I'm trying to get to.

I was a teenager in the 1990s. By the time I finished art school I felt like I'd missed subculture: it was gone, or it'd been taken. Everything had become commodified, there was no 'sub', there was just a mass of different lifestyle options – there was nothing below or above or external to that. There was a feeling, I think, of ennui. I'd gone to art school thinking I was going to write manifestos – you know, I wanted to like, change the world. I studied moving image, I had a structural-film, understand-your-means-of-production kind of education. It was post-Marxist. I remember thinking the means of production isn't paint, or a canvas, it's not even a 16mm film: it is the institution. So then how to know that as a means of production? There was a fantasy of going into the institution and changing it from the inside, a binary fantasy. I followed this path. It is a fantasy because in moving into being that institution, or working within whatever institution, of course what I didn't realise was that I'd become that institution. And so at that time the project became not one of criticising an external force, but more self-reflexive. I became more interested not in what the concrete physicality of the institution was, and criticising that in some sort of site-specific way, but in pursuing a project of understanding how *I* was instituting, and what my role in instituting was – how I worked, not what the work *was*. And that became a different project, one of setting up what a practice would be along those parameters. How can I work differently? How can I generate something differently? How do I understand, not what I am, but *how* I am? How do I understand the action and verb of *practise*, not the product and objects of *practice*? So when I think about institutional critique, if I can't even be critical of my own institution, I don't think I can very well be critical of somebody else's. I became conscious of my own prejudices in making art and how I police the standards. I carry so many prejudices about what a work should be, how it should behave, what it can do – it's incredible, the amount of prejudices that I have. I'm trying to acknowledge and work with those, trying to acknowledge my complicity in the perpetuation of those things. And that also allows me a lot more agency, because the other option is to spend my time lobbying other institutions to change.

During the production of this show, I had just become a mother. I was fighting hard to separate that part of myself. But after a while, actually letting all of that in became part of the full process: acknowledging those limits, recognising and loving those limits even, and trying to work with them. It's not just about the history of art, but about living conditions. The trust that both parties, the museum and me, put in the process of the score, you can feel it, it's incredible. Sometimes, no matter what you say, as an artist how you actually behave is different. But I trusted here, and I am happy to see that full-throttle.

I think that the art industry is finally beginning to acknowledge – hopefully more than at just an optical or representational level – the need for other voices to be heard. The voices of people who do not come from, say, a position of privilege or a position of, I don't know, being able to work in a certain way: many of them have limitations on how they work, whether that's financial, social, physical, emotional. So those practices have to work in different ways. It is important to say this is the way those practices have always had to work: it is not new. I believe those ways of practising are beginning to be acknowledged as valid. It's not through the industry's validification or canonisation of those practices, but the strength of artists recognising: I am valid, what I do is valid, it does not work in the same conventions, my practice doesn't look like that, the work I produce doesn't look like something already known or valorised. But I am going to hold the position of trying to make whatever this precarious form is sustainable for myself. It's different from maybe ten years ago, when I feel like there was always this thing of people entering the canon, of being taken in: suddenly you were acknowledged, or whatever. Whereas this is something else, coming more from artists themselves. Many artists get burnt out, and eaten up – and not just artists: people, directors, curators, they just get destroyed. Any type of industrial process will do that, because it's an extractive model. The point now would be that these practices, by virtue of their limitations, and which use those limitations as material, can be allowed to model some of the other systems around us on their premise.

In the age of narcissism holding a mirror up does nothing at all. There's a different way of modelling self-reflexivity that isn't to do with mirroring, but some other form of self-reflexivity that is more like: What are my actions? What am I doing? Not, What do I look like? It's not retinal, and that's different. For me, and I can only talk personally, that has reassigned how I think about a critical project. I think otherwise it becomes tautological, it's a press release about press releases, or a wall about a wall – it becomes a hall of mirrors that just bounces infinitely in an echo chamber. How you calibrate that reflexivity differently is significant for art-making, for our community. What am I doing? Why did I presume that? What have I set up as the parameters?

We learn how to behave. The way we look at shows, how you go in and you look at *this* for a certain amount of time, and then you look at *that*. There is this specific way we move through space and look at things that's not recognised as something inherited, but it's something I actually remember learning to do. When you first go to galleries, you're like: How do I do this? – and you learn how to do it, and then you become an 'expert'. And then, because you hold this expertise, you want to show others that you hold it. There's a whole performance to it. I think that in the moment you recognise that, you have a chance to do something else. What can be written into existence differently? How can I move differently through these spaces? I don't really get how so many people who talk about being privileged feel like they have to be quiet, or say nothing – like they've spoken too long, or spoken too much. If you have privilege, use it to do something. We need more voices, more people with more resources to mobilise – no matter that you might be implicated. Your silence won't protect you.* And if you don't use the energy that you have, somebody else will, probably for something way more nefarious. That is, you will feel used.

There's a false premise of objectivity or distance, when you're, in fact, completely enmeshed within the industry. I love the

* See of course Audre Lorde, 'The Transformation of Silence into Language and Action', *The Cancer Journals* (San Francisco: Spinsters/ Aunt Lute, 1980), 18–23.

documentary *Chronicle of a Summer* by Edgar Morin and Jean Rouch, a political documentary partly set at a dinner party. The ethnographic lens is turned back onto him, on Paris in the 1960s, it is remarkable for that. Many documentaries tend to centre on elsewhere. I never understood why the context had to be outside. Why was it always somewhere else, when all the politics are here, my politics, which I can speak about? To go somewhere else would be presumptuous. It's here. It's here in this room. We're the ones perpetuating it. We're also the ones who can change it. Now is a good time to act. This is the context, and this is the place that I have an ability to act within – an obligation, even.

The reason people are extracted from is because they have resources, not because they don't. This is how the project of extraction works culturally. I need to recognise my capacity to act rather than trying to find someone to give me that resource or agency, otherwise you become alienated from your value while allowing others to accrue from it. I feel like I only physically realised this when I became a mother: I was struck by how my ability to reproduce and provide care was assumed. I remember when my daughter was just born my partner said, I want to support you as much as I can, I want to buy you as much time as possible so you can keep working. I realised he was not providing me with time, he was not liberating me, I was already buying him the time, giving him the ability to work in the first place. There is no isolation from the entanglement. And there's no isolation from it here in the museum either, because we are here. Even in our isolated times we more and more sense the absolute impossibility of it. In the UK during COVID, it was: Don't go to work, stay in your house, get your shopping delivered – but delivered by who? Someone who's leaving their house. This is the foundation of our society.

I think one of the things I've been trying to figure out is how to retain intimacy, my life, in the work without it becoming an autobiographical commodity. As an artist when your identity becomes almost objectified like the work, as an art object, well,

I don't know, I think that's potentially problematic, because then your identity becomes the commodifiable form and needs to be maintained. I make commodities. I'm aware of that. But how do you do it without identity becoming mythic. How the works circulate, how I have worked with distribution, this has something to do with the diaspora, the negotiation of my mixed identity. Assimilating what I feel deeply as the illegitimacy of my practice and position into a visible, legitimate form – I don't think this is tolerable for me any longer. And I am not willing to turn back now.

I am thinking about porosity, and trying not to segregate or compartmentalise parts of my life: I have to let the material that's around me in. And so this is why I use the material I do, because it's the material that is around me. For example this little *Onions* painting has been around me for a long time. And I sat with it, thinking, What is this thing to me? I was interested in what would happen if I let it in. It's this small oil painting that was in our house in London throughout my childhood, and was always known as 'the onions'. The painting was part of a collection of works that was passed to my maternal grandmother by her aunt Julie Elias, who was married to the German-Jewish art historian and translator Julius Elias. Julius died prior to the outbreak of World War II and in 1938 Julie and their son Carl Ludwig fled Germany to Norway, with much of the Elias collection having been sold under duress in flight from persecution. Neither Julie nor Carl Ludwig survived the war, she died in Lillehammer, he was sent to Auschwitz, and afterwards my grandmother sold the works in order to pass funds back to the remaining family members. The painting we had in our house was a replica commissioned by my grandmother before she sold the original, which was actually by Renoir.

I realised it was not original as a teenager and there was something in that that was felt as a loss, a disappointment for me and a shame for my family. Something to be hidden or forgotten. From then I'd always thought of it as secondary, *less than*. It had this secondary status. So I was interested in what would happen if I let that in, again trying to flood, I suppose. This comes back to historically unvalorised positions in the art world, which have always been there, now beginning to be acknowledged, but that have always been held and validated by their producers. *Onions* is not about questioning secondary status, it's about questioning primary status. This replica and story is enough, it does not need to be re-made as primary to have force and meaning. It can be what it is, to me: onions – because we always thought it was onions, even though the Renoir painting is of pomegranates.

To have the copy of *Onions* re-enter Germany and be exhibited in Germany is beautiful. My family fought to get rid of their German nationality in order to be safe in the UK, and now I'm trying to get back German nationality in order to have freedom of movement in the EU. And so to have this painting circulate again, because of its secondary status, not because of its primary status or its relation to primary status, is something, even in my own head, where the maths doesn't work. Something I don't understand is going on. It's much too small for the exhibition space. Maybe it also speaks to how I feel about being in these spaces. Everyone gets traumatised by this stuff, making a show in a space, it's incredibly public, and you have to deal with issues of intimacy and being seen.

What is in a museum is also what was defined as having validity. Market validity, historical validity, they go hand in hand. In a way, the only thing that *isn't* art is this painting of onions, although I have named it as art, so it is art. It has a more complicated relationship to authority and authoring. Everything else is more clearly my work. But what's interesting is not whether something is or isn't art – what's interesting is the fluidity around it, a transformation that occurs in allowing in what we don't consider as valid. I'm not interested in translating one thing of status A to having status B – what I'm interested in is movement. A kind of movement that makes me question within myself what is important to me. The moment you abandon some of the colonial, postcolonial, neoliberal project of value, then there arises this question of, What is the value we're preserving? What should we preserve? Is preservation even about preservation? There's an assumption that society is progressive, but could you think about the museum in a different way, as the necessary maintenance of historical, critical actions? Could you think about artworks as critical actions to instate value that is not tangible?

Move one thing from the foreground and the background comes into focus, then remove one thing from the background and the foreground comes into focus. And that focus-pull for me creates a movement in my own judgement, in my own way of coming towards things. It is like when the camera lens is making a noise because it can't automatically focus. I don't know if anyone else has that in looking at the work, but I'm trying to do that for myself. I'm trying to create a critique of my own prejudgements at least. I think I've internalised many prejudices in this field. I have been taught to bolster arguments, to defend my position and create a watertight argument. Watertight. That's exactly it. Impenetrable to anybody else. How can you make something discursive if everything is watertight? In this exhibition I was being conscious of this wish in me, and it surprises me, this flood. It's still acting. It's acting. It's not in stasis.

Enough.

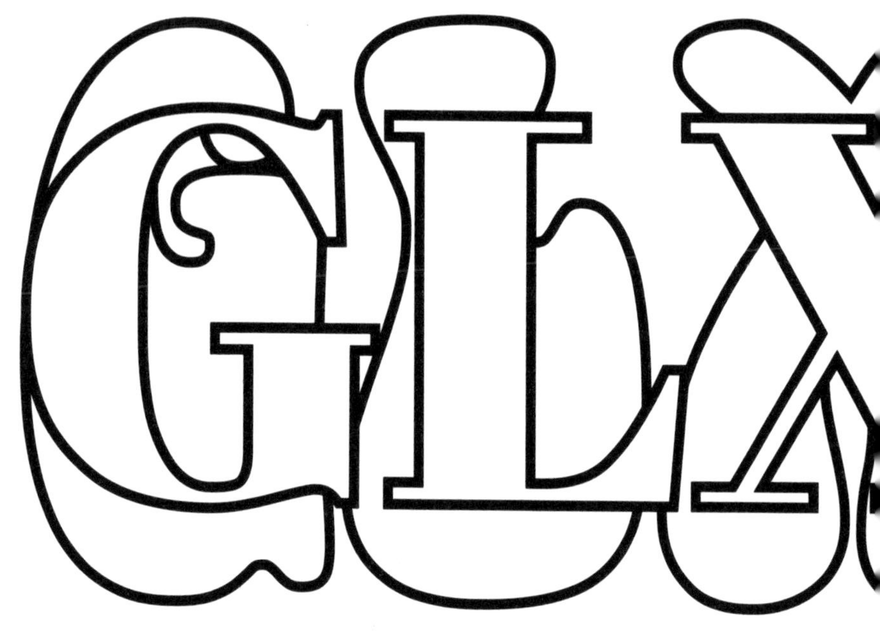

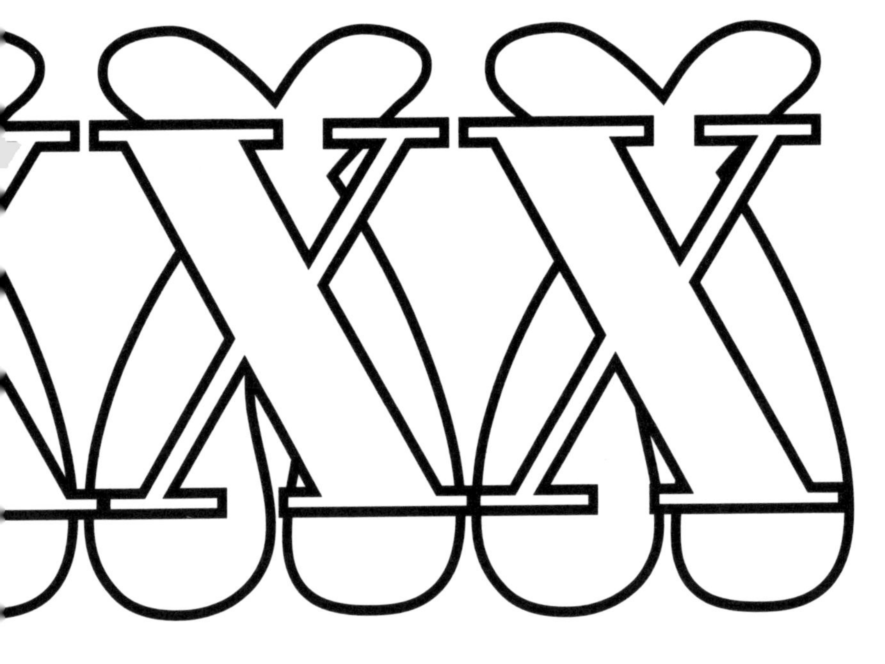

The predominance of neoliberal metric and proprietary logics are underlined by a rampant need for the positive, the measured and the metric, and so able to be validated, pre-validated, and ultimately securitised and monetised as assets. The palpable, rather than say the strictly invisible, sits awkwardly within this criteria. It is felt but not necessarily able to be data-captured. What is perhaps radical is not necessarily the new, but the extant made present. The incidental foregrounded. What might these forms of palpability proffer, how might they question what is inside the pre-validated forms of image distribution?

The algorithm, in its deployment by capital, has parameters that set operations to specific for-profit goals. Often attempts towards radical solutions hinge on the latter, the efficiency of the solution, and as such are too often able to be subsumed into metric logics. Fundamental to the production of alterity must be the capability to produce the unknown, to generate, to de-create, to be unproductive. Scores, synonymous with composition, are ways to generate: they are constitutively mutable and informal, contingent on their performance. What might be written to maximise such contextual contingencies?

Beyond the premise of a transgressive work, if it is the material conditions of labour that produce value as opposed to the object in and of itself, consideration must be made of a transgressive way of working. Risk algorithms are deployed to minimise waste, to maximise efficiency and profit margins. What is not capable of being justified, measured, nominalised and identified, cannot be exercised. How can we work with rigour but without pre-validated criteria? What does this produce?

Swim Group C stayed in the shallow end of the pool, waist-deep in the water, surrounded by floats, in multiple armbands. All the children in Swim Group B trained for certificates in pyjamas and did widths across the pool. All the children in Swim Group A executed dives off the high board and did non-stop lengths. In the changing room a child from Swim Group C was covered in talcum powder until 'white'.

Replace the word 'algorithm' with 'the runes' in all pieces of broadcast news journalism.

Blue broken grey-footed barriers weakly tied together with string and loosely arranged around a concrete single-person bench, one end open rendering the entire structure defunct.

Striped blue and white shirt with green embroidery, curled bleached shoulder-length hair, smoking a cigarette while looking in a small black zipped bag and holding, on the forearm, a nylon Minnie Mouse tote bag which displays multiple black-white red-bowed Minnie heads around a central Minnie figure.

The sound of German.

The London accommodation centre, lettings and estate agents, properties managed, tel: 020 8985 8991. Houses, flats, rooms. Always available. All caps.

Wilting orange stems and dark brown stalks set against pink-painted pebbledash and large front-mounted TRIAX satellite dish.

A country-wide scale process of recladding.

Schedule 1 – map of the Prescribed Area. The Prescribed Area is the area marked out with a red boundary in the map below. N110A Power of Arrest. Above, tied into the black-painted railing with green string, two pairs of keys, one with two keys, one with one key. All rusty.

An abandoned copy of *NIN: Nine Inch Nails* by Tommy Udo, lying on top of a folded blue and white nautical striped multiple-pocket storage organiser. Some distance away, a dried-up water-bloated copy of *The Fountainhead* by Ayn Rand.

Broken bed bases.

The moon at 9.35 a.m.

Drive boy dog boy, dirty numb angel boy.

Semi-peeled-off and re-stuck sheets of protective plastic wrap hanging creased and folding in the windows of a new-build property.

The sudden condensation of time felt as a brick-weight slab on the nape of the neck. In sunshine.

My inability to accountably take decisions, specifically risk-related decisions, vectored against my greed.

Discounted tubs of individually wrapped chocolates.

Unable to watch *George Clarke's National Trust Unlocked* without imagining everything covered in blood.

Someone rehanging the shop sign for the shop Crisis.

Twenty-four per cent year-on-year increase in the cut-flower market.

Two identical artificial miniature red-rose-bush balls approximately thirty centimetres in diameter, suspended on aluminium link chain, hooked into rusted-steel decorative armature, screwed either side of a landscape uPVC window.

Two blue furry plush toy teardrops, wearing underpants, replete with three-dimensional noses, two-dimensional smiling open mouths, and large oversized spectacles positioned roughly upon the noses and over non-existent fur eyes. The left tear wears very large red plastic glasses, the right one small yellow plastic sunglasses and looks away from the other tear, who, sightless, has collapsed, slightly forward.

Singing in a car, all windows open while transporting a heavy wooden coffee table in the farmhouse style.

SELF-INSTRUCTION. Dappled sunshine, cold.

The grey polished composite stone worktop surface is cold against my ankles, almost a heat, it has the form of heat. It radiates. Or heat radiates out from me into it.

Pre-post-rain light. The grass an unnatural hyper-green, over-contrasted. Assorted local borough vehicles; better homes, greener spaces, cleaner borough, enforcement. I'm eating granola. A woman with a Tesco bag. Three women pushing an empty buggy. Granola has fallen all over my legs. I am wearing a bandana and glasses, running leggings, a Peking University T-shirt bought for me by my dad and a loose-weave oversized black cotton knit jumper. A white van with green recycling motif. A bus advertising food drop-offs. A grey van with eagle motif advertising security services. A supermarket van advertising carrots with the phrase, Live well for less. A taxi advertising coffee. A bakery van advertising bread. Yesterday we spoke to our friends about children. Purple leggings, a grey crop-top hoodie.

Dark-purple-red variegated green-flocked velvet leaves spilling up to the dim grey light, budded.

The negotiation of limits in my work is about trying to undo a certain dialectic of value, trying to understand the thing I have or don't have as a resource, trying to understand the situation I'm in as already a resource. As enough.* I have a fantasy or speculation that I should be unlimited, and a projected notion of what unlimitedness should look like in a daily practice or in an exhibition space. Within that fantasy limits are perceived as a hinderance – my financial ability, my need for stable employment, my commitment as a mother, my body, my political efficacy. But those limits, those dependencies could be turned around to become a resource for making artwork in another way, in a way that you don't know what it's going to do. And I constantly have to decide to maintain this turn.

Whatever projection you have about how you should be working as an artist is definitely an internal one. It's about understanding how the material conditions of your situation have consequences. 'I have to function in a way that goes against my hormones, that makes it seem like I'm always the same.' 'It won't work if I don't work sixteen hours a day.' This is my default way of seeing things; then there is my inability to be able to work on the same terms as that fantasy. Maybe it's not working *because* you work sixteen hours a day. Maybe there is fear of the point of internality or reflection that that space might produce. I want to understand the inactive forms of life; it's not necessarily best

* What follows was largely put together from transcriptions of conversations with Divided between January and June 2023.

that you are always in the visible, active form of production. It's about not operating on the basis of external validation.

If you think about financial autonomy as a way of being supported, you can also think of other things as support. What I'm describing are not limits but life, other forms of life that are not your art-industrial life. I have dependents, friends, family, outside the parameter of my artist identity. Do I think of my daughter as a limitation? She's not a limitation, she's my life. I don't want – politically, emotionally, psychologically – I don't want to see this as a limitation. I disagree that suffering is indicative of being a good artist. I'm not saying I'm not perpetually in a situation of crisis.

UK Egg Statistics
UK Slaughter Statistics
Alcohol and Late Night Refreshment Licensing England and Wales
Retail Sales in Great Britain
Insolvency Statistics
A Level and Other 16–18 Results
Characteristics of Children in Need
Children Accommodated in Secure Children's Homes
Outcomes for Children Looked After by Local Authorities (LAs)
Pupil Absence in Schools in England
School Workforce in England
Children in Care in Northern Ireland
Fostering in England
Absenteeism from Primary Schools
Absenteeism from Secondary Schools
Violence at Work: Findings from the Crime Survey for England and Wales
Drug Misuse: Findings from the Crime Survey for England and Wales

Firearm and Shotgun Certificates in England and Wales
Police Powers and Procedures in England and Wales
Seizures of Drugs in England and Wales
Deaths during or following Police Contact in England and Wales
1990/1991 Gulf Conflict UK Gulf Veterans Mortality Data: Causes of Death
UK Armed Forces Compensation Scheme Statistics
UK Armed Forces Deaths in Service
UK Armed Forces Suicide and Open Verdict Deaths
War Pensions Scheme Annual Statistics
Civil Justice Statistics Quarterly
Criminal Court Statistics Quarterly
Family Court Statistics Quarterly
Mortgage and Landlord Possession Statistics
Prison Population Projections
Proven Reoffending Statistics
Race and the Criminal Justice System
Women and the Criminal Justice System
Safety in Custody Quarterly
Legal Aid Statistics in England and Wales
Youth Justice Annual Statistics
Mortgages: Actions for Possession Bulletin
Focus on Property Crime
Focus on Public Perceptions of Crime
Focus on Violent Crime and Sexual Offences
Fraud and Computer Misuse Statistics for England and Wales
Homicide in Scotland
Air Passenger Duty
Alcohol Duty
Betting, Gaming and Lottery Duties
Child Benefit Statistics Geographical Analysis
Corporation Tax Statistics
Individual Savings Accounts Statistics
Inheritance Tax Statistics
Tobacco Duty
Public Spending Statistics Release

Index of Production
Index of Services
Profitability of UK Companies
Adult Inpatient Survey
Community Mental Health Survey
Maternity Services Survey
Report on Abortion Statistics in England and Wales
Cancer Waiting Times
Accidental Deaths
Alcohol-related Deaths in Scotland
Deaths from Various Causes
Drug-related Deaths in Scotland
Healthy Life Expectancy in Scotland
Hypothermia Deaths
Probable Suicides: Deaths Which Are the Result of Intentional Self-Harm or Events of Undetermined Intent
Winter Mortality in Scotland
Prescription Cost Analysis, England
Adult Dental Health Statistics
Adult Psychiatric Morbidity Survey
Breast Screening Programme, England
Cervical Screening Programme, England
Children's Dental Health
Data on Written Complaints in the NHS
Guardianship under the Mental Health Act
Mental Health Act Statistics, Annual Figures
National Child Measurement Programme
Obesity, Physical Activity and Diet
Sexual and Reproductive Health Services, England
Smoking, Drinking and Drug Use among Young People in England
Statistics on Alcohol, England
Statistics on Smoking, England
Alcohol-related Deaths in Northern Ireland
Adult Drinking Habits in Great Britain
Alcohol-related Deaths in the United Kingdom
Avoidable Mortality

Cancer Statistics Registration, England
Child Mortality in England and Wales
Excess Winter Mortality in England and Wales
Health State Life Expectancies
Pregnancy and Ethnic Factors Influencing Births and Infant Mortality
Suicides in Great Britain
Trends in Life Expectancy by the National Statistics Socio-Economic Classification
Unexplained Deaths in Infancy, England and Wales
Geographic Patterns of Cancer Survival in England
Abortions Statistics, Termination Statistics
Cancer Incidence
Cancer Mortality
Cancer Survival Statistics
Cancer Waiting Times
Care Home Census
Complaints Statistics
Infant Feeding Statistics
National Drug and Alcohol Treatment Waiting Times
Place of Death from Cancer
Suicide Statistics for Scotland: Update of Trends
Teenage Pregnancies
Unintentional Injuries
Eye Care
Maternity: Method of Delivery
Housing Statistics
Affordable Housing Supply in England
Social Housing Sales in England
UK House Price Index
Homelessness in Scotland
Affordable Housing Provision
Deliberate Fires
Homelessness: Annual Release
Social Housing Sales
Trade Union Membership
English Indices of Deprivation

Average Household Income, UK
Family Spending in the UK
Gender Pay Gap in the UK
Household Debt in Great Britain
Household Income Inequality, UK
Labour Disputes in the UK
Low and High Pay in the UK
Total Wealth in Great Britain
Working and Workless Households in the UK
Young People not in Education, Employment or Training, UK
Poverty and Income Inequality in Scotland
Public Sector Employment in Scotland
Freedom of Information Statistics
Babies' First Names
Births Time Series Data
Deaths Time Series Data
Childbearing for Women Born in Different Years, England and Wales
Divorces in England and Wales
Marriages in England and Wales
Drinking and Driving
Road Lengths and Conditions
Road Safety
Road Traffic
Sea Transport
Young People Road Casualties

This practice isn't something that's done. It's a maintenance act, it's something I maintain in myself against something else. It has to have that relational framework, it's idiosyncratic and subjective. Whatever myth I've internalised is not going to be yours, that's yours to change. I believe how I've internalised that system and how you have internalised the system can be changed, but you need a lot of help to do that. It's not something I could have got to on my own, it's a product of community and history and luck and conversations like this. If I was off by myself I wouldn't have got there. There's a projection in competitive society that everyone else can run to it and keep up. But if intimacy occurs there's a moment when that competitiveness disappears into a moment of solidarity. Art is an immense psychological risk. It's hard to take that risk without support.

I want to create an identity where not all is carried on an industrial, functional infrastructure, based on labour and market. In different contexts I'm different things. I'm Jewish and I'm Chinese. I'm also neither, because I'm not a practising Jew and I don't speak Chinese and I never met my Chinese family. I'm also British, but am I really? Your coherence is based on whether you can trade as a certain commodity. I could be that commodity, I could do that high-functioning neoliberal labour, but why is that what commitment is? I don't want that. Commitment could be something else. So then, what boundaries can I set up against that unlimited self that I'm supposing I should function as? If I'm my own boss, maybe I should start to acknowledge the limitations, rather than trying to overcome them? Are they even limitations? Maybe they are just things I care about? Without which I would perish.

There isn't always a break. The becoming broken can be incremental. An extruded break, stretched out and curled up inside. That extends pre-birth and past death, to be so long and loud and pitched so high and violent as to be mute.

A flamenco-style peach-red slack-hanging too-big dress, plastic leather mules, filled cloth tote shoulder bag.

I can see hiding, I can see what hiding allows and also what I give up in doing it. It's like a cryptic safety, after a while that palatable kind of safety itself becomes intolerable. The crisis is the performance, an endless flexibility to any situation. Constantly performing to succeed, a flexible personality. If I could stop coping could there not be something better? I learnt that to stop performing like this, that is the practice; to exist and show yourself with that unknown. Let something die, a notion of who you are. Let the notion of work, or what your work is, go. Let something else come through, make space for a different kind of work.

A cloud of yellow hair simplified into a basic shape surrounding a grinning pink-tan face, also simplified and without any nose, wielding a parcel in the left hand aloft the head, the other hand empty but celebratory, printed tall over the side of a long-wheelbase delivery van.

A bag that, due to the strain upon the plastic, its weight and handle placement, now just reads HELP.

Pressurised rubber tyres compressed against grey flooring under the weight of an entirely child-filled seat and multiple disposable bags, attached to cheap thin plastic or metal foldable structure. The neck of the child slumped forwards into zipped jacket.

Santander bikes.
Weaning products.
Soft top cars.

The bloom of perfume or aftershave, of warm skin, intimacy and contagion.

The capacity to inflict pain conflated in some kind of never-ending curve chart with the desire for control.

Numbers.

Virality.

Why is it easy to love the oppressor not the oppressed?

My father watched *My Fair Lady* seven times before moving to the UK from Hong Kong in 1970. I'll say it again, assimilation is a violence. I didn't know there was a test but apparently I pass.

The artwork needs you, your life, your labour, this voice. Don't use analogy or metaphor to stay clean, instead feel it and say it as it is and then be okay with discomfort. Let be what is already there: feelings, expectations, awkwardness, beauty, shame. Don't ask others to validate your position, it will undermine the radicality of a position held without validation. Performing at home, hiding at school then hiding at home, performing at school. My challenge might be to find a way where I am neither hiding myself nor performing myself. It's hard enough to find the challenge, and then you start practising it. I have the capacity to act, so I can stop looking for someone to give me that.

What I am interested in is practice and how people are practising. The ones I really love are ones I feel as full-on life practices, Hanne Darboven, Julie Becker, Lee Lozano, full vibrational porosity of the materiality of life and work. Ego death. Can you understand the labour in that? To the point of – in their cases – near-obliteration. I found it very hard to say, I am an artist. I couldn't say it. Because I thought about it as a title, an identity title, I am an artist, that somehow the name meant you are the thing. Now I think about it in the action of, the commitment to, and the maintenance of making artwork, within the framework of doubt of what and who you are. For a long time I thought you had to get over that doubt to be an artist. But I have to go into it, so deep into it that I am blind in its condition. I've stopped trying to overcome this condition that I feel is actually constitutive of the work, the life. I used to think the conditions of production were located in the gallery, not in life.

The repetitive motion of cigarette hand to mouth, followed by can hand to mouth. Three people walk past up the steps and no eye contact is made. Small pooling mounds of leaves, assorted refuse plastics, dirt. The entrance is cut back into the building and boarded to one side. Wider at the front than back. It narrows to a green secured-entry door.

Floral micro-skirt, grey added-Lycra denim jacket, blazingly white Converse Chuck Taylor All-Stars, mid-sized gold-coloured hoop earrings.

The sweet smell of frying minced meat, sticky onions, water slowly releasing.

I get paid 21.24 GBP per twenty-four-hour day, seven days a week for my job in the care industry. This is allocated for thirty-nine weeks, after which I will get nothing and no provision to work elsewhere without paying to do so. Implicit in the conjecture that I must buy myself free, is that I was born into debt.

Translucent semi-opaque frosted double-glazed panel blurring several objects in mint green, white, grey, royal blue, red, and shaped oblong, round and circular.

My mother was born in 1943.

High-contrast soft-focus wet light. Slimy flattened hairs on pulsating belly in aforementioned light.

Partner Look.

A car so compressed as to look toy-like.

Scattered light on leaves in a flux of colours that only ever exist related to each other and by dint of their proximate situation, under over above and in motion. It sounds of waves. The aching surround sound of vibrating substances alive.

The cold small curl of your hand in mine.

The impromptu architecture of satellite dishes.

The confluence of extreme poverty and inequality and the sudden emergence of narratives on space travel, in a three-dimensional graphic rendered in motion and looping infinitely. A Mario's-brother-like figure appears atop the largest peaks and does a little dance.

Assorted hearses.

White platform trainers.

Incredibly long hair kinked from the neck down and bouncing mouse-coloured against the back and extending to touch the top of the legs.

Three women in various fitted leather-look black jackets in motorcycle and biker styles.

Little children being thrown in the air. Little children standing supported on the bonnets of parked cars. Little children having haircuts.

Light tan thin-fabric trousers, pale mauve-grey jacket, red across-the-body bag, a beige hat, white socks, black loafers.

A huge close-cropped image of carrots with a curled handwriting-style text stating LIVE WELL.

A white and glass funeral carriage followed by four black SUVS and a pest-control van. All slow-moving.

I'll say it again. It is my favourite thing to swim naked in the dark, blind and blurred, not only myself and all shattered fluid into stars and salt water.

Ghislaine Leung is a British conceptual artist. Born in Stockholm, Sweden to a father from Hong Kong and a mother from London, she was raised first in Reims, France and then in London, UK. She received a BA in fine art in context at the University of the West of England in 2002 and a master's in aesthetics and art theory at the Centre for Research in Modern European Philosophy at Middlesex University in 2009. Between 2004 and 2014 she worked at Tate and LUX, London. Leung's first book was *Partners* (Cell Project Space, 2018). She lives in London.